Eleventy by Example

Create powerful, performant websites with a static-first strategy

Bryan Robinson

BIRMINGHAM—MUMBAI

Eleventy by Example

Copyright © 2023 Packt Publishing

Group Product Manager: Pavan Ramchandani

Publishing Product Manager: Bhavya Rao

Senior Content Development Editor: Feza Shaikh

Technical Editor: Simran Udasi

Copy Editor: Safis Editing

Project Coordinator: Aishwarya Mohan

Proofreader: Safis Editing

Indexer: Hemangini Bari

Production Designer: Alishon Mendonca

Marketing Coordinator: Anamika Singh, Namita Velgekar, Nivedita Pandey

First published: May 2023

Production reference: 1060423

Published by Packt Publishing Ltd.
Livery Place
35 Livery Street
Birmingham
B3 2PB, UK.

ISBN 978-1-80461-049-7

www.packtpub.com

To my wife, Emily, this book would not exist without your support, patience, love, and belief in me. To my son, Lincoln, you change my perspective each day; thank you for being you.

– Bryan Robinson

Contributors

About the author

Bryan Robinson is a developer and designer with over 15 years of experience building and leading teams on the web. He enjoys well-written HTML, clean CSS, and just the right amount of JavaScript.

I want to thank the whole of the 11ty community. The folks that work on and around 11ty are some of the nicest, most supportive developers on the internet. I've always enjoyed 11ty but watching the creative applications of those in the community keeps my passion fresh.

It also may go without saying, but none of this would be possible without Zach Leatherman, the creator of 11ty. When I learned about this little framework, it was like learning that Zach had read my mind and created something specifically to help me author websites in the exact way I'd always wanted to. To this day, I've yet to find a framework, language, or system that I enjoy using more.

About the reviewers

Ed Henderson has over 25 years of experience in full stack web design and development. He has witnessed the evolution of web technologies, from the early days of HTML and CSS to the latest cutting-edge frameworks and tools.

Throughout his career, Ed has had the opportunity to work on many projects in the UK, Europe, USA, and Asia, collaborating with diverse teams and clients from different backgrounds and cultures.

Ed now lives in East Lothian, just outside Edinburgh, with the rest of team Hendo: his amazing wife, Rose, and awesome sidekicks, Jack, Toby, and Noah.

Saad Koubeissi is a senior frontend software engineer from London, United Kingdom. With over a decade of industry experience, he is currently working as an engineering manager. Saad combines his love for accessibility and UX while adhering to web standards to build performance-driven websites and applications. Eleventy (11ty), React, and Next.js are among his favorite tools. As an avid supporter of mentoring, Saad has volunteered for various programs and organizations, such as The Duke of Edinburgh's Award, coaching young learners through Harvard's prominent computer science (CS50) course. Beyond working as an engineer and mentoring, Saad is the co-founder and co-host of the "Life in Tech with Jay and Saad" podcast.

Table of Contents

3

Deploying to a Static Site Host   29

4

Building a Blog with Collections   43

5

Creating Custom Shortcodes to Add Mixed Media to Markdown   63

6

Building a Photography Site with the 11ty Image Plugin   79

7

Building a Podcast Website with 11ty Plugins and Custom Outputs   95

8

Creating a Static-Site Search with 11ty Serverless and Algolia   105

Preface

Eleventy (11ty) is the dark horse of the Jamstack world. In the tradition of **static site generators** (**SSGs**) such as Jekyll and Hugo, 11ty takes steps to bring the entirety of the Node.js ecosystem to help developers build highly performant, static-first websites that can be served blazingly quickly from a content delivery network (or simple server).

Eleventy by Example covers everything you need to create your first 11ty website, then dives into making more complex sites and extending 11ty's base functionality with custom shortcodes, plugins, and content types. Over the course of five interactive projects, you'll learn how to build basic websites, blogs, media sites, and static sites that still respond to user input without needing a server. With this, you'll learn about basic 11ty concepts such as templates, collections, and data use, and advanced skills such as plugin creation, image manipulation, working with a headless CMS, and using the powerful 11ty Serverless plugin.

By the end of the book, you'll be ready to take advantage of all the power 11ty offers to build almost any web project, with best practices that can be taken from project to project, reducing the time it takes to get a site launched.

Who this book is for

This book is for anyone who is looking for ways to ship less JavaScript to the client to create more performant sites while still providing a strong developer experience. You should have a strong knowledge of HTML and CSS and at least beginner knowledge of JavaScript and the Node.js ecosystem, including querying APIs.

What this book covers

Chapter 1, Setting Up Your Website, what is 11ty? This chapter dives into the world of SSGs to explore why 11ty exists and gets you started on your path to creating static-first websites with simple templates and configuration.

Chapter 2, Adding Data to Your Website, in this chapter, we take the project created in *Chapter 1* and extend it by employing multiple techniques to import data into our HTML. We will learn all about the 11ty Data Cascade and how to add static and dynamic data.

Chapter 3, Deploying to a Static Site Host, a site isn't a website until it's been deployed to a server. In this chapter, we'll take a look at the requirements for getting your 11ty website deployed to a static site host.

Chapter 4, Building a Blog with Collections, now that you've deployed your first 11ty website, let's create a new project. In this chapter, we'll dive into the world of 11ty collections to create a basic blog with custom templates, pagination, and dynamic category pages.

Chapter 5, Creating Custom Shortcodes to Add Mixed Media to Markdown, a blog isn't just text. Sometimes you want more interactive elements. In this chapter, we'll extend the basic functionality of 11ty to add custom shortcodes to import YouTube videos, CodePen displays, and custom blockquotes with semantic HTML.

Chapter 6, Building a Photography Site with the 11ty Image Plugin, images can provide an amazing amount of interest to your website. In this chapter, we dive into the 11ty Image plugin to discover how our static site can have optimized images for both a user's browser and for our image's use case.

Chapter 7, Building a Podcast Website with 11ty Plugins and Custom Outputs, not everything a website needs is HTML. In this chapter, we'll take a look at the unique needs for a podcast website and output both an HTML website and a standards-compliant podcast RSS feed to launch your very own podcast.

Chapter 8, Creating a Static-Site Search with 11ty Serverless and Algolia, when you reach a certain level of content, search is an inevitability. Without a server, creating a search functionality is often relegated to frontend code. With 11ty Serverless, we can have solid, progressively enhanced search experiences without needing to create a split in our code base.

Chapter 9, Integrating 11ty with a Headless CMS, markdown is great for many content use cases, but sometimes you just need a **content management system** (**CMS**). In this chapter, we see how 11ty can work with the headless CMS Hygraph to provide a great editor experience alongside a great developer experience.

Chapter 10, Creating Custom 11ty Plugins, throughout this book, we've customized 11ty in many ways. Needing to do that customization between projects can require a lot of copying and pasting. In this chapter, we'll optimize our flow by creating three custom 11ty plugins that give us great power for each of our projects.

To get the most out of this book

This book assumes a passing familiarity with beginner knowledge of Node.js, HTML, and CSS.

Software/hardware covered in the book	Operating system requirements
11ty 2.0	Windows, macOS, or Linux
Node.js 18	Windows, macOS, or Linux

If you are using the digital version of this book, we advise you to type the code yourself or access the code from the book's GitHub repository (a link is available in the next section). Doing so will help you avoid any potential errors related to the copying and pasting of code.

Download the example code files

You can download the example code files for this book from GitHub at https://github.com/ PacktPublishing/Eleventy-by-Example. If there's an update to the code, it will be updated in the GitHub repository.

We also have other code bundles from our rich catalog of books and videos available at https:// github.com/PacktPublishing/. Check them out!

Download the color images

We also provide a PDF file that has color images of the screenshots and diagrams used in this book. You can download it here: https://packt.link/ERy5P.

Conventions used

There are a number of text conventions used throughout this book.

Code in text: Indicates code words in text, database table names, folder names, filenames, file extensions, pathnames, dummy URLs, user input, and Twitter handles. Here is an example: "This HTML is now on every page using the base.html layout."

A block of code is set as follows:

```
{% if title or bannerContent %}
<section class="banner">
  {% if title %}<h1>{{ title }}</h1>{% endif %}
  {% if bannerContent %}<p>{{ bannerContent }}</p>{% endif %}
</section>
{% endif %}
```

When we wish to draw your attention to a particular part of a code block, the relevant lines or items are set in bold:

```
return {
    dir: {
        input: "src",
        output: "_site", // This is the default, but it's included
here for clarity.
        includes: "_templates"
    }
}
```

Any command-line input or output is written as follows:

```
npm install @11ty/eleventy@v2
```

Bold: Indicates a new term, an important word, or words that you see onscreen. For instance, words in menus or dialog boxes appear in **bold**. Here is an example: "For this demo, we'll use **Rich Text** to get additional options in our API."

> **Tips or important notes**
> Appear like this.

Get in touch

Feedback from our readers is always welcome.

General feedback: If you have questions about any aspect of this book, email us at customercare@ packtpub.com and mention the book title in the subject of your message.

Errata: Although we have taken every care to ensure the accuracy of our content, mistakes do happen. If you have found a mistake in this book, we would be grateful if you would report this to us. Please visit www.packtpub.com/support/errata and fill in the form.

Piracy: If you come across any illegal copies of our works in any form on the internet, we would be grateful if you would provide us with the location address or website name. Please contact us at copyright@packt.com with a link to the material.

If you are interested in becoming an author: If there is a topic that you have expertise in and you are interested in either writing or contributing to a book, please visit authors.packtpub.com.

Share Your Thoughts

Once you've read, we'd love to hear your thoughts! Scan the QR code below to go straight to the Amazon review page for this book and share your feedback.

https://packt.link/r/1804610496

Your review is important to us and the tech community and will help us make sure we're delivering excellent quality content.

Download a free PDF copy of this book

Thanks for purchasing this book!

Do you like to read on the go but are unable to carry your print books everywhere?

Is your eBook purchase not compatible with the device of your choice?

Don't worry, now with every Packt book you get a DRM-free PDF version of that book at no cost.

Read anywhere, any place, on any device. Search, copy, and paste code from your favorite technical books directly into your application.

The perks don't stop there, you can get exclusive access to discounts, newsletters, and great free content in your inbox daily

Follow these simple steps to get the benefits:

1. Scan the QR code or visit the link below

https://packt.link/free-ebook/9781804610497

2. Submit your proof of purchase

3. That's it! We'll send your free PDF and other benefits to your email directly

1
Setting Up Your Website

At its core, **Eleventy (11ty)** is a simple concept. It takes a group of pages, data, and templates and combines them to create a static output – typically HTML – that can be served on a web server or distributed on a **content delivery network (CDN)**. Tools that do this are typically referred to as **static site generators (SSGs)**.

In this chapter, you'll learn all you need to know to get your first simple 11ty website completed. In order to do this, we'll talk a little bit about the history of static sites to uncover what makes 11ty special, as well as how to install and configure it on your computer to get moving in a simple, best-practice-focused structure. Every 11ty concept starts with the concepts in this chapter. This is what we will cover in this chapter:

- What are static site generators and why are they important?
- What is 11ty?
- Running 11ty with no configuration
- Configuring 11ty with basic best practices
- What's the difference between a page, a template, and a layout?
- Creating the base layout file
- Setting up pages and templates
- Creating reusable includes

Technical requirements

In every chapter in this book, you'll need a computer with Node.js and npm (11ty is built with Node.js and runs via npm), a code editor such as VS Code, and access to the book's GitHub repository for both the starting point code and the finished work. 11ty's minimum required Node.js version is 14. The code for this book was written and tested with Node 18. Basic knowledge of HTML, CSS, JavaScript, and the command line will also be beneficial.

Before beginning, fork and clone the project's GitHub repository: `https://github.com/PacktPublishing/Eleventy-by-Example`.

What are static site generators and why are they important?

SSGs have been around since early in the history of web development with systems such as **HSC** (which stands for **HTML Sucks Completely**) and **Movable Type** looking to solve the sometimes problematic developer experience of authoring plain HTML for multi-page sites. These technologies added features such as **includes** and **macros** that made creating and maintaining HTML websites much easier.

The other direction development began to move in was rendering templates on the server instead of serving simple HTML back per request. The upside to this was a strong developer experience and the ability to create pages dynamically. Templates were created and uploaded to a server and when a request came from a client, the pages' HTML was built and sent to the client. This methodology would become the predominant authoring experience for the web over the next decade. With it came longer load times.

SSGs would see a boost in 2008 with the creation of **Jekyll**, a Ruby-based SSG created by *Tom Preston-Werner*. Preston-Werner was the co-founder of GitHub, and by the end of 2008, Jekyll would power GitHub Pages, allowing developers to create and host websites through their GitHub repositories. The method of pre-building HTML and serving it directly from a web server instead of building pages at request time leads to improvements in performance and security over what had become traditional web development. To this day, Jekyll is still one of the leading SSGs owing to the integration with GitHub Pages. To extend Jekyll, however, required a stronger knowledge of Ruby, something not every developer knew. That's where 11ty came in.

What is 11ty?

11ty is an SSG developed by *Zach Leatherman* in 2017 with a strong sense of inspiration from Jekyll but built in the then-flourishing JavaScript ecosystem. If you know a little Node.js or JavaScript, you can extend the functionality of 11ty. If you don't have a strong JavaScript background but can run a few commands in the command line, you can use 11ty.

11ty has a few strong philosophies:

- **Static-first** – While there are new features in 11ty that allow it to run at request time, as well as pre-generate HTML, the strongest use of 11ty will be to create a static site first, and then extend into the server rendering only when necessary.

- **Flexible** – 11ty doesn't prescribe one way to create sites. In fact, one of the strongest benefits of 11ty over other SSGs is that it comes bundled with over 10 templating engines that can be used separately or together.

- **Frontend agnostic** – 11ty doesn't force you into a single frontend framework. 11ty's task is creating HTML pages – how you extend that into client-side JavaScript is up to you and not tied to the framework. How you accomplish frontend interactivity is completely up to you, from what framework you choose to what toolchain you use. Things are completely decoupled.

With this basic understanding of 11ty, it's time to run it for the first time.

Running 11ty with no configuration

While most sites you build with 11ty will require some amount of configuration, 11ty comes packaged with enough defaults to get you up and running without writing any configuration.

To start, from within the cloned GitHub repository, open `project-1/chapter-1/start` in your code editor. This project has a very basic HTML website. It has an `assets` directory with CSS and images and an `index.html` and `about.html` document with some basic structure and content. If you open `index.html` in a browser, you'll get a web page, but it won't have any styles associated and the anchor to the About page won't work. That's because this page is expected to run on a server.

Installing 11ty

In order to get a local server, we'll install and run 11ty.

First, all Node.js projects need a `package.json` file. We can create one by running the following:

```
npm init -y
```

Running this command will initialize this project as a Node.js project and create a `package.json` file with the basic defaults needed. Next, we need to install the 11ty package:

```
npm install @11ty/eleventy@2
```

Now, the project has access to the `eleventy` command. For simplicity, add two scripts to the `scripts` object in `package.json`. This not only makes it easier to run locally but also will help when it's time to deploy this site in *Chapter 3, Deploying to a Static Site Host*:

```
"scripts": {
  "dev": "eleventy --serve",
  "build": "eleventy"
},
```

The `dev` script runs 11ty in `serve` mode, which gives us a local server with live reloading – great for developing – and the `build` script creates the site that we can upload to a CDN or server. These two commands are all that is needed to make 11ty work for this project.

Running 11ty

Throughout this book, we'll primarily run 11ty in `serve` mode. Running `build` will create nearly the same output but won't run a local server and provide live reloading. The following command will also be used to generate files for hosting later:

```
npm run build
```

```
> eleventy --serve

[11ty] Writing _site/index.html from ./src/index.html (liqui
d)
[11ty] Writing _site/about/index.html from ./src/about.md (l
iquid)
[11ty] Copied 1 file / Wrote 2 files in 0.07 seconds (v2.0.0
)
[11ty] Watching…
[11ty] Server at http://localhost:8080/
```

Figure 1.1 – 11ty running in the console

The terminal will give information on what 11ty is doing after running the `build` command. There should now be a new `_site` directory in our project. Inside that directory is the `built` HTML that 11ty put together. Now, instead of an `about.html` file, there should be an `about` directory with an `index.html`. This is 11ty converting the HTML file into a *pretty* URL for final use. The `index.html` file should reside in the root of `_site`, creating the home page for the site. Both pages should be identical to what is in the original files.

The terminal output will also display the URL for accessing the local version of this server. 11ty defaults to `http://localhost:8080`.

When you click that link, the site still won't have CSS, but the navigation should now work. To get CSS functional, we need to configure 11ty.

Configuring 11ty

While 11ty can be run without configuration, a little configuration will make our project cleaner and give us access to additional functionality within 11ty.

To configure 11ty, in our project root, we need a configuration file: `eleventy.config.js`. At its core, 11ty is a Node.js project. The 11ty configuration file is a JavaScript file that exports a configuration function.

The basic structure of the file is as follows (not project code):

```
// Create variables that require() any packages we need
const plugin = require('some-eleventy-plugin-package')

// Use module.exports to export a configuration function
module.exports = function(eleventyConfig) {
  // Run any code needed (including built-in 11ty methods)

  // If needed, return an object of configuration
  return {
     // Options here
  }
}
```

By default, 11ty does not keep track of CSS files, basic JavaScript files, or image files. To get the CSS into our build, 11ty needs to be told to copy those files into the final build. In the `eleventy.config.js` file, add the following code:

```
module.exports = function(eleventyConfig) {
    // Copy `assets/` to `_site/assets/`
    eleventyConfig.addPassthroughCopy("assets");
}
```

The `addPassthroughCopy()` method accepts a string that matches a directory in the project. In this case, this is the entire `assets` directory. This `addPassthroughCopy()` method will tell 11ty to copy that entire directory over to the `_site` directory and name it the same. After making this change, the CSS should now function, as it is being linked in the HTML pages to `/assets/style.css`.

After making most changes to the configuration file, a restart of 11ty's server is required. In your terminal, hit *Ctrl + C* to stop the process and then run `npm run dev` again. Once the server restarts, your styles should be working.

Further configuration

There are many options for modifying 11ty's behavior via this configuration file. All the options are documented in 11ty's documentation. This book will dive heavily into many of those options, but some are for special use cases. They're all worth investing a little time to understand and read.

While this is all that's necessary to get the static assets copied over, we can also use this opportunity to configure the project to have a cleaner structure. 11ty defaults to keeping everything stored in the project root directory, but it can be a little overwhelming. A best practice is often to move the main files that 11ty uses into a subdirectory, often named `src`.

Figure 1.2 – Example directory structure with an src directory

First, move the index.html and about.html files into a new directory called src. This should result in the site no longer working. Don't worry, this is only temporary.

Next, adjust the eleventy.config.js file to return an object from the exported function. Inside this object, add the dir object and specify an input property with the src string. While unnecessary, this code example also shows how to adjust the output directory for consistency and readability:

```
module.exports = function(eleventyConfig) {
    // Copy `assets/` to `_site/assets/`
    eleventyConfig.addPassthroughCopy("assets");

    // Set the source for 11ty to the /src directory
    // Otherwise, this defaults to the project root
    // This provides a cleaner project structure
    return {
        dir: {
            input: "src",
            output: "_site" // This is the default, but
                it's included here for clarity.
        }
    }
}
```

Once this update is saved, the site should build properly again. For most of the work in this book, the src directory structure will be how we structure the projects. Templates, pages, and data will all reside within this folder.

Understanding the difference between a page, template, and layout

One of 11ty's strengths is also a source of confusion. 11ty comes bundled with 10 templating languages. These languages (including Liquid, Nunjucks, and Handlebars) can be used to create individual pages, includes, and layouts, and can be chained together to create complex systems. While this is incredibly powerful, it can create confusion around terminology.

The 11ty documentation says that layouts *"are special templates that can be used to wrap other content."* This doesn't necessarily clear things up. For this book, we'll use the following definitions to try to keep things clear:

- **Page** – an item meant to be rendered as a single URL on the final site, for example, `index.html` or `about.html` in this project

- **Layout** – a file that is used by a page to wrap content in the entire structure for an HTML page

- **Include** – a file consisting of a small, reusable amount of code that should be shared by multiple pages or layouts

- **Template** – includes or layouts

With the vocabulary out of the way, we can create and use our first layout.

Creating the base layout file

Up to this point, everything we've accomplished with 11ty can be replicated in other, smaller tools. Removing the basic HTML boilerplate from each page makes the code much more maintainable and extensible.

To start, we need a new subdirectory in the `src` directory. Name this directory `_templates`. By default, 11ty uses an `_includes` directory for includes and layouts. To avoid semantic confusion, we'll update our configuration to use the new directory instead.

> **A note on directory naming**
>
> It's perfectly fine to use the default folder names. Most of my 11ty projects use the `_includes` naming convention. This step is more for clarity than best practices.

In the configuration function's `return` statement, update the `dir` object to include an `includes` property:

```
module.exports = function(eleventyConfig) {
    // Copy `assets/` to `_site/assets/`
    eleventyConfig.addPassthroughCopy("assets");
```

```
// Set the source for 11ty to the /src directory
// Otherwise, this defaults to the project root
// This provides a cleaner project structure
return {
    dir: {
        input: "src",
        // This is the default, but it's included
        // here for clarity.
        output: "_site",
        includes: "_templates"
    }
}
}
```

All of the templates 11ty will use will be stored in this directory. Inside the new directory, create two additional directories: `includes` and `layouts`. This level of separation isn't necessary for 11ty to work, but keeping includes and layouts separate will continue building clarity in your project.

Inside the `layouts` directory, create a file named `base.html`. This will become the main layout for use on the site.

```
 1  <!DOCTYPE html>
 2  <html lang="en">
 3    <head>
 4      <meta charset="UTF-8" />
 5      <meta http-equiv="X-UA-Compatible" conten
 6      <meta name="viewport" content="width=devi
 7      <title>My amazing title</title>
 8      <link rel="stylesheet" href="/assets/css/
 9    </head>
10    <body>
11
12      <header class="site-header">
13        <svg
14          width="46"
15          height="15"
16          viewBox="0 0 46 15"
17          fill="none"
18          xmlns="http://www.w3.org/2000/svg"
19        >
20          <g clip-path="url(#clip0_1_2)">
```

```
 1  <section class="banner">
 2    <h1>This is my homepage banner</h1>
 3    <p>This is my banner content</p>
 4  </section>
 5
 6  <section class="triptych">
 7    <div class="triptych__item">
 8      <h2>Triptych 1</h2>
 9      <p>Triptych 1 content</p>
10    </div>
11
12    <div class="triptych__item">
13      <h2>Triptych 2</h2>
14      <p>Triptych 2 content</p>
15    </div>
16
17    <div class="triptych__item">
18      <h2>Triptych 3</h2>
19      <p>Triptych 3 content</p>
20    </div>
```

Figure 1.3 – The original index.html next to the new version of index.html

Inside this file, we'll take the reusable sections from `index.html` and place them here. This includes all the meta information from the HTML document – `DOCTYPE`, `html`, and `head` elements – as well as the main `header` element from the page (containing the SVG logo and navigation). Once the top section is moved, we also need the footer area and the closing body, and `html` tags. The only thing left in `index.html` should be content that is specific to that page.

In between the top portion and the footer of the new base template, we need to insert a spot for each page's unique content to be inserted. We can do that via the `{{ content }}` template tag:

```html
<!DOCTYPE html>
<html lang="en">

<head>
    <meta charset="UTF-8">
    <meta http-equiv="X-UA-Compatible" content="IE=edge">
    <meta name="viewport" content="width=device-width,
        initial-scale=1.0">
    <title>My amazing title</title>
    <link rel="stylesheet" href="/assets/css/style.css">
</head>

<body>
    <header class="site-header">
        <svg width="46" height="15" viewBox="0 0 46 15"
            fill="none" xmlns="http://www.w3.org/2000/svg">
            Content omitted for brevity </svg>

        <nav>
            <ul>
                <li class="active"><a href="/">Home
                    </a></li>
                <li><a href="/about">About</a></li>
            </ul>
        </nav>
    </header>

    {{ content }}

    <footer class="footer">
        <p>Copyright 2022</p>
    </footer>
</body>
</html>
```

What's this {{ }} doing in my HTML?

If you're already familiar with templating languages such as Liquid and Nunjucks, feel free to skip over this section. If you've never worked with separate template engines, this syntax is from Handlebars, Liquid, and Nunjucks – three engines that are shipped with 11ty.

By default, 11ty will render any file that ends in `.html` with the Liquid template engine. Anecdotally, most projects in the 11ty ecosystem use either Liquid or Nunjucks as their primary engine, so learning a bit about either is good in the long term. Both Liquid and Nunjucks share quite a bit syntactically and practically. Here are the basics you'll need to know in this book:

- `{{ myObject.myVariable }}` – Display the value of a given variable in data. Liquid refers to these as variables, and Nunjucks refers to them as expressions. Their use is the same.
- `{% tag %} {% endtag %}` – Tags are either paired and used for things like loops and conditionals, or singular and used for things like assigning values to variables.

Most of this book is written to use Liquid, as it's the default in 11ty and doesn't miss too much functionality in comparison with other engines. With that said, 11ty's flexibility is one of its superpowers, so I encourage you to explore the differences in all the engines and see which one fits your workflow the best. While you'll often use only one language per project, any project can use any number of engines. To convert a Liquid template to a Nunjucks template, you can simply change the file extension to `.njk`, and as long as you're not using any Liquid-specific tags or filters, 11ty will automatically update to the new engine for that file.

What happened to the head and footer?

If you saved the `index.html` file, you may have noticed that your site no longer has those reusable components. That's because we haven't updated the index page to know what layout to use.

To do that, we need to provide a little data to the page. Page-specific data is often added as **frontmatter** at the top of the file. We'll cover additional ways of adding data in *Chapter 2, Adding Data to Your 11ty Website*, but frontmatter will be important throughout the book.

Frontmatter is a YAML block at the top of a file. This is a standard convention across many SSGs. To add a YAML block, add a paired set of `- - -` at the top of a page and then provide key-value pairs to create data for that page.

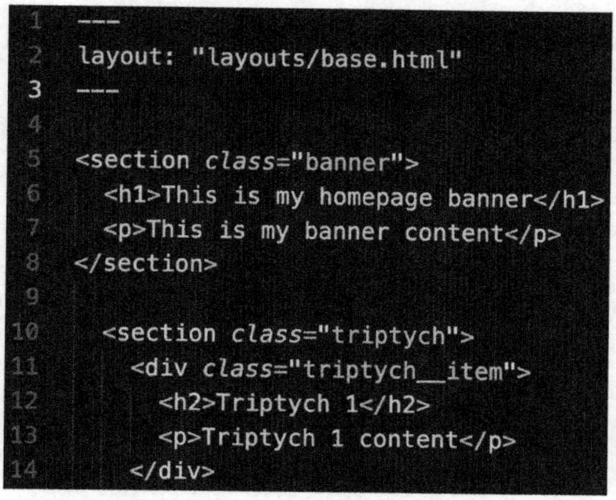

```
1   ---
2   layout: "layouts/base.html"
3   ---
4
5   <section class="banner">
6     <h1>This is my homepage banner</h1>
7     <p>This is my banner content</p>
8   </section>
9
10    <section class="triptych">
11      <div class="triptych__item">
12        <h2>Triptych 1</h2>
13        <p>Triptych 1 content</p>
14      </div>
```

Figure 1.4 – The index.html page with frontmatter

The data is only available for that specific page or template. To attach a layout to the page, we provide the `layout` key with a value of a file path relative to the `_templates` directory we selected for our templates. In this case, we'll add the following code to our `index.html` page:

```
---
layout: "layouts/base.html"
---
```

With this update, the content left in the `index.html` page should now flow into the correct spot in the layout and the page should render properly.

Fixing live reload

A browser refresh is necessary at this point. While much of the development in 11ty will cause the browser to refresh on its own through 11ty's new development server, we broke that connection by removing the HTML boilerplate from that page. The development server requires a `<head>` element on the page to work, so at this point, you'll need to refresh the browser to see updates, then the live updating will work again.

From here, update the `about.html` page the same way. Once both pages use this layout, any change you make to the layout will be reflected on both pages. This makes maintaining simple HTML much more reasonable.

Now that we have a well-structured project and layout, let's break the HTML into reusable chunks called **includes**.

Creating reusable includes

While the base layout is more maintainable, we can make it easier to reconfigure by breaking the layout down into smaller pieces called includes. These includes will be the beginning of taking the code and turning them into building blocks that can be remixed into different layouts as necessary.

To start, we need to identify the smaller pieces of the base template. Let's create a header.html file in the src/_templates/includes directory and move all the HTML meta information and visible site header into that file. Everything from the DOCTYPE element to the header element should be removed from base.html and moved into the new file.

While we're refactoring the header, let's also move the <nav> element into its own include, as well. 11ty templates can be nested. This means we can include files inside other files. In this case, the header.html include can include navigation.html.

Create a navigation.html file in the includes directory, as well, and move the entirety of the navigation into that file. This will make the navigation reusable. This could be used in the footer or other areas where additional site navigation could be useful.

The HTML in base.html should be replaced by a Liquid include tag:

```
{% include "includes/header.html" %}
```

The header.html include should include the following code (note the nested include):

```
<!DOCTYPE html>
<html lang="en">
<head>
    <meta charset="UTF-8">
    <meta http-equiv="X-UA-Compatible" content="IE=edge">
    <meta name="viewport" content="width=device-width,
      initial-scale=1.0">
    <title>My amazing title</title>
    <link rel="stylesheet" href="/assets/css/style.css">
</head>
<body>

    <header class="site-header">
        <svg width="46" height="15" viewBox="0 0 46 15"
          fill="none" xmlns="http://www.w3.org/2000/svg">
        /* removed for brevity */
        </svg>

        {% include "includes/navigation.html" %}
    </header>
```

The footer is also ready for abstraction. Create a `footer.html` file in the `includes` directory and add the `footer` element and closing `body` and `html` tags into it:

```
<footer class="footer">
  <p>Copyright 2022</p>
</footer>
</body>
</html>
```

At this point, the only items that should be left in `base.html` should be two includes – `header.html` and `footer.html` – and the `{{ content }}` variable. There are two more elements that seem ideal for abstraction: the home page banner and each of the three promotional cards beneath it – a pattern often called a **triptych**. The problem is that these elements are currently hardcoding their content. If we abstract the page banner and want to use a page banner on the About page, we would need to change the content, and each triptych item needs to have unique content for each promotion.

This is where even more power in 11ty is unlocked. We'll cover the data cascade and the various methods to include data in your templates in *Chapter 2, Adding Data to Your 11ty Website*.

Summary

In this chapter, we took a basic HTML website and converted it to an 11ty site. We learned about the philosophies and terminology that are core to understanding 11ty. We ran 11ty with no configuration, then set 11ty up with a best-practice structure using 11ty's `eleventy.config.js` configuration file. We repurposed our HTML code into reusable layouts and includes for maintainability and reusability.

To take this chapter further, look at how you might break the `header.html` include down into smaller, more readable pieces. Maybe abstract out the meta tags into their own `include` or move the logo SVG into its own file.

In the next chapter, we'll take a look at 11ty's powerful Data Cascade and how to add dynamic or unique data to each `include` as well as to our pages and layouts.

Further reading

- Full 11ty configuration documentation: `https://www.11ty.dev/docs/config/`
- CloudCannon's history of static site generators: `https://cloudcannon.com/blog/ssg-history-1-before-jekyll/`

2

Adding Data to Your 11ty Website

In the last chapter, we set up the basics of an 11ty website. In this chapter, we'll give it superpowers by exploring the many ways that 11ty allows us to add static and dynamic data to our templates, layouts, and pages.

At the heart of any website is data. Whether that's content, structured data, or third-party information, getting data onto a page is the most important thing any site generator can do. By adding a data layer to the simple website we built in *Chapter 1*, we'll see how the flexibility of 11ty extends to data via its Data Cascade feature, and how this provides us with great power for customizing our various layouts, includes, and pages.

In this chapter, we'll be covering the following topics:

- Understanding the 11ty Data Cascade
- Adding data for each page
- Adding data to external files
- Adding global data

Technical requirements

The code in this chapter builds on the site that we built in *Chapter 1*. If you didn't follow along with that chapter, you can find the complete code in the companion GitHub repository: `https://github.com/PacktPublishing/Eleventy-by-Example/tree/main/project-1/chapter-2/start`.

Understanding the 11ty Data Cascade

Before we can dive into the code, we need to discuss how 11ty handles data.

Much like 11ty's template options, the way 11ty handles data is also very flexible. With that flexibility comes some extra complexity. 11ty allows you to add data at every layer of your project, in page files, layout files, directories, and globally. Based on that, there's a specific order and precedence in which it ingests the data along the way. This is called the 11ty **Data Cascade**. Let's take a look at data sources in order of highest priority to lowest priority. At each step along the way, data can either be merged or overridden.

Lowest-priority, most generic data—such as a global data file—is the first to be computed. This gives us access to that data to be used or mutated by higher-priority, more specific data—such as computed data.

Computed data

While we won't cover computed data in this chapter, it is the data with the highest priority and the last to run. 11ty computed data is run at the page or template level and has access to various data variables that are already available. It can be used for things such as generating page permalinks, working with the navigational structure, or anything else that requires additional data to be already compiled.

Page frontmatter

We covered the frontmatter a little in *Chapter 1* as a way of declaring what layout our pages will use. The frontmatter can also be used to add page-specific data to each page template. Examples include titles, publish dates, descriptions, and data required for the page, such as banner content and promotional space content.

Template data files

Template data files are specific files of JSON or JavaScript data that are paired by name with specific pages. This can make for a better developer experience than just using frontmatter data on an individual page. These data files need filenames that match the template name.

Directory data files

Directory data is shared between multiple pages in a specific directory in your project. This can be used to share things such as layouts and parent IDs between various pages within a section of your site. For deeply nested directories, the data from parent directories is also available within the deeply nested template. This data file needs to match the directory it lives within.

Layout frontmatter

Layouts in 11ty are just chained templates. So, any page or layout can have frontmatter. In the context of a layout, the frontmatter is the same as a page, but a page can override its layout. The layout frontmatter can be helpful for creating template inheritance features to show different data on each section of your site based on the layout.

Configuration API global data

You used the 11ty configuration API to set up your 11ty instance in *Chapter 1*, but it can also be used to store global data. The `addGlobalData` method on the configuration object can be used to create regular global data but is best used to create data source plugins for various APIs and add data programmatically to the 11ty data stack.

Global data files

The lowest-priority data is global data. These files are typically JavaScript or JSON files and are stored by default in the `src` directory of your project. This data is accessible to any template, layout, include, or page in your project. These files are great for data that should be fetched or created once and used in multiple places.

With the basics in hand, let's begin by making our templates and includes more dynamic. To start, we'll add individual page data that can be used in our base template, as well as in includes.

Adding data for each page

The home page of our website has a large banner at the top. It would be great to be able to reuse the HTML from that banner on the About page as well. If we move the HTML from the home page into an include and use it in both places, the headline and banner text will be identical. That's where page data comes in.

Adding variable data to the home page

In the `index.html` file, we already have the YAML frontmatter that we used when setting up the layout in *Chapter 1*. This is where the page data lives.

To add additional variables, we can follow the same format as we use for the `layout` variable and add a new line to the frontmatter. This time, add a `title` and `bannerContent` variable. Each of these will contain a string that will be used by the templates:

```
---
layout: "layouts/base.html"
title: "This is my homepage"
bannerContent: "This is my banner content"
---
```

These two new variables are accessible inside of the page, the layout controlling the page, and the includes that are included on the page.

To start, replace the static HTML in `index.html` with Liquid variable expressions, as we discussed in *Chapter 1* for the `{{ content }}` variable. Any variable entered into the frontmatter of a page is accessible by the key given to it:

```
<section class="banner">
    <h1>{{ title }}</h1>
    <p>{{ bannerContent }}</p>
</section>
```

Now that we have the content as data in our page, we can move the HTML from the page into an include placed in the base layout.

Copy the markup from the home page and move it into a new file named `banner.html` in the `src/_templates/includes` directory. Your directory structure should now be updated.

Figure 2.1 – banner.html should now be in the includes directory

No noticeable changes should happen on the home page. Once the file is added, we can include `banner.html` in the `base.html` layout file with the following code:

```
{% include "includes/banner.html" %}
```

At this point, we can modify the About page to handle the same data.

This HTML is now on every page using the base.html layout. That means we have access to it on the About page as well as the home page. Right now, there's no data, so the h1 and p elements will appear on the page but will be empty. We'll update the About page with the proper data in a moment, but let's first add protections against pages that don't have this content.

Writing conditionals to display no markup if data doesn't exist

To protect our HTML, we need to add conditionals to our include. We need to think about three different cases:

- When there is no title or bannerContent, don't display the entire section
- When there is no title, don't display h1, but display the bannerContent paragraph
- When there is no bannerContent, display h1, but not the bannerContent paragraph

Most conditional operators you may be used to from other languages are also available in Liquid (and Nunjucks). For the first case, we need to check whether either title or bannerContent exists; for the second case, we need to check whether title exists; and for the third case, we need to check whether bannerContent exists:

```
{% if title or bannerContent %}
  <section class="banner">
    {% if title %}<h1>{{ title }}</h1>{% endif %}
    {% if bannerContent %}<p>{{ bannerContent }}</p>
      {% endif %}
  </section>
{% endif %}
```

This adds all the protections we need. Now, the About page no longer has a blank banner at the top. But we *do* need a banner, so let's update the About page.

Adding About page data and content

When we created the About page in *Chapter 1*, we set it up to use base.html like the home page. Because it's using that layout, we now have access to the same banner include if we provide the same data structure to the page frontmatter. By adding the same data to the About page's frontmatter, we can have a custom banner:

```
---
layout: "layouts/base.html"
title: "About us"
bannerContent: "This is a little paragraph about the
  company."
---
```

The page should now display a banner across the top, but let's take this one step further. While it makes sense to keep the home page as an HTML document, authoring long-form content isn't easy in HTML. While the frontmatter may be structured data, we can also use other types of content data in our pages. Let's convert the page from HTML to Markdown—a more ergonomic way of authoring structured content in code.

To do this, change the file extension from `.html` to `.md`. By default, 11ty will read that as a Markdown document and use Markdown and Liquid to generate HTML from it. This means that all valid HTML and Liquid tags work in the page's code, as well as standard Markdown syntax:

```
---
layout: "layouts/base.html"
title: "About us"
bannerContent: "This is a little paragraph about the
  company."
---


## The page content can go here

It can use any markdown, since we're in a markdown page. Like [an
anchor](https://packtpub.com) or **bold text**.

* Or an unordered list
* With some items

1. Or an ordered list
1. With some items (no need to have different numbers in a
   Markdown ordered list)
```

Now we have structured page data and our page content is transformed into data, but let's take this a step further and create unique styling for the home page banner compared to the About page banner.

Typically, a home page banner will be styled with more padding and take up more space compared to an interior page, where getting users to the content faster is important.

To accomplish this, we need to dynamically add a class to the home page banner to modify its styles. Let's add a `pageId` variable to the frontmatter of the home and About pages. For the home page, set it to home, and for About, set it to `about`.

Then, we can modify the banner include to add a class when `pageId` is home. We can do this with another Liquid conditional, this time checking the value of `pageId` rather than just whether it exists:

```
{% if title or bannerContent %}
  <section class="banner{% if pageId == "home" %} banner—
    home{% endif %}">
    {% if title %}<h1>{{ title }}</h1>{% endif %}
```

```
    {% if bannerContent %}<p>{{ bannerContent }}</p>
      {% endif %}
  </section>
{% endif %}
```

We add `banner--home` as a class in the section when it matches home; otherwise, it's just `banner`. This matches the class in the CSS file to set a `min-height` on the banner. If you want to take this a step further, you could use the `pageId` value itself and set styles for every page ID in your CSS.

> **Whitespace**
>
> Note the whitespace choices in the class list. There's no space between `banner` and the conditional and there's a space preceding `banner--home`. This is intentional and will render the HTML with no awkward whitespace. If you don't mind extra spaces in your source code, you can choose to accommodate that space before the conditional. I care more about the rendered markup than perhaps I should.

We can also use `pageId` to set an active state on our navigation to show users what section in the navigation the current page is in.

To do that, open the `navigation.html` include we created in *Chapter 1*. For each navigation list item, we can create a conditional to check which `pageId` is in use and display an `active` class for the proper navigation item:

```
<nav>
    <ul>
        <li {% if pageId == "home" %}class="active"
          {% endif %}><a href="/">Home</a></li>
        <li {% if pageId == "about" %}class="active"
          {% endif %}><a href="/about">About</a></li>
    </ul>
</nav>
```

Now that we have a working navigation and About section, let's expand on the home page by adding data for a standard web design pattern—the triptych.

Adding an array to the frontmatter and looping through it in a page

We've drastically simplified the About page and applied reusable components between pages. The home page still has a section that has a lot of repeating HTML. The triptych area—three identically styled cards next to each other—has the same markup, but different content for each card.

We could put three sets of uniquely keyed data in the home page frontmatter and write the HTML around that, but it would be better to write the markup once and allow the data to be looped through and render the repeated HTML. To do this, we can use a YAML array and a Liquid `for` loop.

Add the following to the frontmatter of `index.html`:

```
triptychs:
  - headline: "Triptych 1"
    content: "Triptych 1 content"
  - headline: "Triptych 2"
    content: "Triptych 2 content"
  - headline: "Triptych 3"
    content: "Triptych 3 content"
```

> **Whitespace part 2**
>
> Note the whitespace again. YAML is whitespace sensitive, so the exact spacing is important.

If we add a dash before the start of each first property, YAML will interpret this as an array. The keys in the array should line up and the next dash will denote the next item in the array.

To use this data, we'll use another built-in Liquid template tag: `{% for %}`.

The `for` tag is a paired shortcode that will loop through an array. It follows this syntax: `{% for <variable-to-store-data> in <array-variable> %}`. This allows you to format your code in efficient ways:

```
<section class="triptych">
  {% for triptych in triptychs %}
  <div class="triptych__item">
    <h2>{{ triptych.headline }}</h2>
    <p>{{ triptych.content }}</p>
  </div>
  {% endfor %}
</section>
```

Let's make this even more reusable. Right now, this works in this space, but what if we want to have this style of item elsewhere? Let's refactor it into an include and transform the data we pass into it so that it works with any data to make a new card. Make a new `include` named `card.html`. Bring the entire `triptych__item` into the new `include` and reference the `include` from within the `for` loop:

```
<section class="triptych">
  {% for triptych in triptychs %}
    {% include "includes/card.html" %}
  {% endfor %}
</section>
```

This works and might feel like we're done, but it will only work with data under the triptych key. To fix this, we can pass specific data under specific keys to the include.

We can extend the previous code snippet to rename each variable as we pass it into the include. We set the headline variable to `triptych.headline` and the content variable to `triptych.content` to give it the proper format for the new include. This way, anywhere we want to use the include, we just pass the correct data to the correct key.

The new `for` loop looks as follows:

```
<section class="triptych">
  {% for triptych in triptychs %}
    {% include "includes/card.html", headline:
      triptych.headline, content: triptych.content %}
  {% endfor %}
</section>
```

The new `include` looks as follows:

```
<div class="triptych__item">
  <h2>{{ headline }}</h2>
  <p>{{ content }}</p>
</div>
```

The frontmatter is a great place to work with simple data, but as you may have noticed, it starts to get very complicated with just a little extra data. Let's make the developer experience a little better by moving the data to an external file.

Adding data to external files

Data in the frontmatter can be helpful for writing content close to the page, but sometimes having discreet data files can keep the page files much cleaner. We can move data from the frontmatter to specific files along the 11ty Data Cascade.

Creating a template data file for the home page triptych

Let's start by moving the triptych data from the frontmatter into a data file for the home page. To create a template data file, we create a file with a specific naming pattern. For JSON files, we use `<template-name>.json` or `<template-name>.11tydata.json`. For JavaScript data files—which we'll dive into later in this chapter—the `11tydata` string is required for template or directory data.

For this example, we'll use a JSON file to store the array we need for the home page. Create a file in the src directory named `index.json`. If you're currently running 11ty, the terminal will show an error that the JSON is not formatted properly. That's because 11ty already recognizes the data file, but it's blank, and therefore incorrectly formatted for JSON.

For the triptych, insert the following JSON into the file you just created:

```json
{
    "triptychs": [
        {
            "headline": "Triptych 1",
            "content": "Triptych 1 content!"
        },
        {
            "headline": "Triptych 2",
            "content": "Triptych 2 content!"
        },
        {
            "headline": "Triptych 3",
            "content": "Triptych 3 content!"
        }
    ]
}
```

Once this is saved, the browser will refresh, and now we have six triptych items! When possible, 11ty will attempt to merge data from various sources instead of overriding it. So, for the triptych key, it knows that there are two arrays and adds them together. Note the template data file's array content comes first. That's because the template data is added first in the data cascade and then the frontmatter is added. If you insert a `title` string into the template data file, you won't see the title change. That's because the frontmatter takes precedence in the cascade and strings won't be merged like arrays.

The array merge is a nice feature, but we don't want six items. For now, delete the frontmatter from the home page. The home page file is now much more readable and more data can be added to the data file and not overwhelm the page template. The same could be done for data for the About page as well. Follow the naming convention with `about.json` and add any data you'd like.

If we had multiple pages with data files for each page, that would be difficult to manage. To fix this, we can use directory data files.

Moving the About page to its own directory

11ty allows for a deeper directory structure in the project to keep things neat but also adds additional power to pages that should be grouped together.

To start, create a new directory in the `src` directory. Name this directory `about` and move `about.json` and `about.md` into it. 11ty will recognize that the `about.md` file is meant to be the root of that directory and automatically uses that file for the `/about/` route on our site. It will also accept `index.md` as the main file for this route. To keep things obvious, let's change `about.md` to the `index.md` filename.

> **A note of caution on filenaming**
>
> While 11ty allows the use of the `about.md` filename, it's often better to go with `index.md` for this file. By using `about.json`, we're telling 11ty to treat the data in `about.json` as *directory data*. If we want template data for the About page, we need it to be `index.md` with `index.json` as the data file. For this example, this is unnecessary, but it can be important for bigger projects with a larger data structure.

The `about.json` file can now provide data for any page within the `about` directory. Let's add a History page to our About section.

Create a new file in the `about` directory and name it `history.md`.

Add some Markdown to the file and save it. When 11ty rebuilds the site, there will now be a route at `/about/history/`. This page will only display the Markdown you added to the file. In order to take advantage of the layout and other data, the layout path needs to be added. Instead of recreating reusable data, let's move certain data to the directory data file. Both the `layout` data and the `pageId` data may need to be used by any page in the About section, so let's add those two pieces of data to the `about.json` file:

```
{
    "layout": "layouts/base.html",
    "pageId": "about"
}
```

Once that's saved, the page will have the header and footer, as well as the correct navigation item selected. We're still missing a banner. To add the banner, create the frontmatter in the History page. This ensures that the banner content is unique for each page:

```
---
title: "History"
bannerContent: "This is a little paragraph to start talking
  about the history of the company."
---


## The page content can go here

It can use any markdown, since we're in a markdown page. Like [an
anchor](https://packtpub.com) or **bold text**.
```

We'll dive deeper into directory data when creating a blog collection in *Chapter 4*.

While this is all good for a set of unique data, it's often important to share data across the entire site—footers, metadata, and more are often powered by global data. Let's add some data for all of our pages and templates.

Adding global data

Page and template data are great when adding unique data. Directory data is great for sharing data between specific pages. But what if you need to add data to every page? That's where global data files come in.

To use global data files, we need a directory to store them. Inside the `src` directory, create a new directory named `_data`—11ty's default data directory name. This can store multiple data files. Each file in this directory will give access to its data to any template using a key with the same name as its filename. For our site, let's add some general site information and add the ability to access it from multiple files.

Create a new file in the `_data` directory named `site.json`. This file will have general information about the site, including the site name and the copyright date to be displayed in the footer:

```
{
    "name": "My Awesome Site",
    "copyright": "2022"
}
```

With this data in hand, let's insert it into our templates.

In the site head—located in `src/_templates/includes/header.html`—we'll update the title. Currently, it's just a hardcoded string. Let's have it pull the page title and the site title:

```
<title>{{ title }} - {{ site.name }}</title>
```

In the footer—located in `src/_templates/includes/footer.html`—let's adjust the copyright information:

```
<footer class="footer">
    <p>&copy; {{ site.name }} {{ site.copyright }}</p>
</footer>
```

Now the information is all changeable from one location whenever it needs to be updated.

Adding dynamic global data

Keen readers will have noticed something slightly off with that last section. The copyright date is already out of date. I'm writing this book at the end of 2022, but you're not reading it then. To change this for the site, we would need to go into our footer each year and change the date. However, 11ty's JavaScript data files can update this for us.

While JSON can be a handy format for simple data, it can be extended by writing it as JavaScript. Any code written in a JavaScript data file will be run each time the site builds. If we update the site's copyright data with a script, it means the site will just need to be rebuilt each year, and no content change will be needed.

> **What do you mean "built"?**
>
> 11ty has no client-side JavaScript code generated by default. Any JavaScript we write for data files will run when the HTML for the site is generated by 11ty—often referred to as "at build time." This happens when the default `eleventy` command is run in the terminal. This usually happens in your hosting provider, but can be run locally as well.

To start the process, let's convert `site.json` over to `site.js`. This will immediately break the running of the terminal process. This is not a proper JavaScript module export.

Since the file is now a JavaScript file, it needs to be refactored to export the object instead of just containing the JSON object.

```
module.exports = {
    "name": "My Awesome Site",
    "copyright": "2022"
}
```

When you run 11ty again, it should work as it did before.

Now that this is a JavaScript file, any Node.js JavaScript can be run from within the file. For our use, we can use the built-in `Date` functionality in JavaScript to get the current date and save the year string as a globally accessible variable named `copyright`:

```
module.exports = {
    "name": "My Awesome Site",
    "copyright": new Date().getFullYear()
}
```

Now, the copyright date in the footer should display the current year instead of 2022. This is a simple example of using dynamic data in 11ty, but anything Node.js can do, 11ty's JavaScript data files can also do. This includes things such as reading files from the filesystem, querying APIs, and transforming data.

Summary

In this chapter, we covered multiple ways of adding static and dynamic data to your 11ty site. After reviewing the structure of the 11ty Data Cascade, we added multiple types of data to our basic site project.

We started by adding page-specific data by using the frontmatter in each of our pages. We used this data to display different content for the banner on the home page and the About page with a singular include. We set up more differences in our layout by assigning a `pageId` inside the frontmatter to display different banner styles and active states in the navigation. We created a reusable card component to be used with data from the home page and renamed it for the include so that it could be used in multiple locations.

Once we had that, we needed to clean up the display of the data in the templates. We used template data files to accomplish this, moving the triptych data to a separate data file with the same name as the page.

We created a new directory for the About section to use directory data files to share data between the About page and the new History page, which is a subpage of About.

Finally, we added global data to display certain information in multiple templates—the site name and copyright date. We started with a JSON file but converted it into a JavaScript data file to pull the current date for the copyright year in the footer.

In the next chapter, we'll discuss the hosting needs of 11ty and walk through deploying a site through a modern static site host.

3
Deploying to a Static Site Host

In the first two chapters, we created a simple website with 11ty. The files generated by 11ty can be served from any web server. They require no special software beyond the ability to serve HTML to a browser. That's part of what makes static site generators so special. In this chapter, we'll explore the strategies for deploying an 11ty site and what hosts are best suited for hosting 11ty websites.

We'll cover how to get the website up in the simplest of terms, but expand upon that to find efficiencies so that the deployment process is fully automated. To do that, we'll find the best hosts for 11ty websites and cover the basic questions to ask to assess each one to find the one best suited to you, as well.

In this chapter, we'll be covering the following topics:

- Technical requirements for hosting 11ty
- Deploying 11ty manually
- Deploying 11ty to Netlify
- Deploying 11ty to Cloudflare Pages

Technical requirements for hosting 11ty websites

11ty builds HTML documents. HTML documents can be served from most web servers. Despite the simplicity of serving files, there are still requirements to keep in mind when choosing a host for an 11ty site.

When choosing a host, ask the following questions to decide whether it's the best fit for your needs and 11ty's needs:

- How will the host build files?
- How are the files served?
- What other services does the host provide?

Let's try answering these questions.

How will the host build files?

As we covered in *Chapters 1 and 2*, 11ty creates HTML files from layouts, includes, pages, and data. To do this, the 11ty package needs to be run via a command-line interface. In this chapter, we'll cover how to run the build process manually to acquire files suitable to upload to a server, but there are better ways to handle this via a *build process*. A build process sees when changes have been made to the production code, runs 11ty, and uploads the built files to the proper place on a server.

Many static site hosts—such as **Netlify**, which we'll cover later in this chapter—have this built in. When selecting a platform, make sure they allow the installation of packages from npm, as that is what is required to run 11ty. Beyond that, most of these platforms will often charge for overages of *build minutes*—minutes spent building your site on their deployment infrastructure. For many small-to-medium sites, this won't be much of an issue and often keeps within free tiers. 11ty is also one of the fastest builds for SSGs—arguably second only to the Hugo SSG.

Other hosts will require a third party such as CodeShip or CircleCI to do the build and then upload it to the server. These third parties will charge for overages on build minutes, as well.

While there's nothing wrong with any of these processes, it's important to think about your workflow during this process. It's often considered best practice to consolidate this process in one ecosystem for simplicity and ease.

How are the files served?

One of the key benefits of 11ty—and most SSGs—is the performance for end users. Serving pre-built HTML from a server is almost always going to offer better performance than rendering the page at request time. That said, there are better ways to serve static files than just hosting them on a server. The best way to host a static site is via a **content-delivery network** (CDN). If your host doesn't provide a CDN, it will be harder to take advantage of the speed a static site offers.

> **Why a CDN?**
>
> No matter how fast the server runs, there is always a limitation in the speed of delivering files: the speed of light. The further from the server a user is, the longer it will take the data to travel. We get around that by hosting the pre-built HTML on servers around the world and deciding at request time which server should serve the files. If that sounds complicated, it is. A CDN does all of this for us, however. When files are built, they're uploaded all around the world to various servers and at request time, the closest file is served.

What other services does the host provide?

For all of their benefits, there are downsides to static sites. Things that require server-side code can't be run on static HTML. Things such as forms, which were relatively easy in server-rendered frameworks, become impossible without third parties in a static site. Because of this, hosts that specialize in static sites offer many additional services to help ease these difficulties. The following is a list of services that can be important for hosting static sites:

- A build workflow (as covered earlier)
- GitHub integration
- Form processing
- Serverless functions
- Environment variable access

After considering these factors, we can look at exactly how to deploy an 11ty site to a host.

Deploying 11ty manually

To start, let's look at how to deploy an 11ty site manually. While there are better options for this process that we'll explore later in the chapter, understanding what is happening is important.

> **A site to deploy**
>
> We'll deploy `Project 1`, which we built in *Chapters 1 and 2*. If you didn't follow that process, get a copy of the files from this book's GitHub repository (`https://github.com/PacktPublishing/Eleventy-by-Example/tree/main/project-1`). Open the project in a code editor and terminal and move into `/project-1/chapter-2/end` for a working 11ty site to deploy.

The main directory of an 11ty project is not what's needed on a server. Most of the files won't serve properly—despite some of them having an `.html` file extension. Before uploading any file, 11ty needs to run in build mode to generate the files needed to upload.

From within an 11ty project, run the following command:

```
npm run build
```

When we installed 11ty in *Chapter 1*, we created a script in the `package.json` file to build 11ty. Behind the scenes, this runs the `eleventy` command with no flags, which will build the site without things such as Browsersync being added or a local server running.

Once that command runs, 11ty will regenerate the `_site` directory—or if this is the first time being run, generate the directory. The contents of the `_site` directory are what need to be uploaded to the root directory of the web server hosting your site. These files can be uploaded via FTP, rsync, or other methods supported by the host you chose. Most hosts that specialize in static sites—such as Netlify—don't offer these options. If you still want to get the `_site` directory live on a server and haven't chosen a platform yet, I recommend using **Netlify Drop**: a drag-and-drop interface to take a directory of static files and put them on their CDN. You can try this at `https://app.netlify.com/drop`.

This isn't the ideal way of hosting on Netlify, however. To make this process smoother, we'll want to use a host that has a deployment process built in to get the files onto their CDNs. For that, we need to set up our project to run properly on a build system.

Let's create our build system for a static site host.

Deploying to a static site host

Whether you choose Netlify, Vercel, Cloudflare Pages, or another platform, the process to deploy to a static site host begins with a GitHub repository.

Setting up a GitHub repository

Whether you're starting from the code you've been working on since *Chapter 1* or coming fresh and using the `end` directory from the GitHub repository, it will be best to move this directory to its own folder on your computer and initialize a new Git repository by running `git init` within the directory.

While the project files have a global `.gitignore`, this new project won't have that available. Before moving forward, add a `.gitignore` file to the root of the new project. In this new file, add the following code to have your repository set up properly:

```
# Keep node modules out of GitHub and have them be fetched
  at build time
node_modules
# The site should be generated in our chosen platform, not
  stored in Git
_site
```

Once the `.gitignore` file is set up, add your files to the repository and make the initial commit with the following commands or via your Git user interface of choice:

```
git add .
git commit -m "Initial commit"
```

From there, log into your GitHub account in a browser, create a new repository, and follow the instructions to connect your local repository to the GitHub repository.

> **New to GitHub?**
>
> GitHub is the industry-standard service for using Git-based version control. If you're new to using Git and GitHub for version control, Packt has a free e-learning course called *Version Control with Git and GitHub* to explain the basics:
>
> `https://www.packtpub.com/product/version-control-with-git-and-github/9781789951141`

Once the repository is set up, it can be connected to a static site host for deployment.

Deploying 11ty to Netlify

Before we start to deploy, let's examine Netlify in terms of the questions we asked at the beginning of the chapter:

- *How will Netlify build files?* Netlify gives a full deployment ecosystem and can run Node.js packages via npm. Netlify also has the ability to have *build plugins*—bits of code that can be installed from their marketplace to perform various tasks at any point during the build process.

- *How does Netlify serve files?* Netlify has a built-in CDN to serve files all over the world.

- *What other services does Netlify offer?* Netlify has a suite of static site services: serverless and edge functions, built-in form processing, environment variable control, analytics, authentication, split testing, branch deploy previews, and more.

To start, you'll need a Netlify account. You can sign up with various platforms such as GitHub or via an email address and password.

Once you have an account, you'll be prompted to deploy your first site:

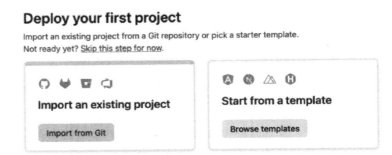

Figure 3.1 – The Deploy your first project page after logging into Netlify. On this
page, you can select whether to import a project or start from a template

Since we already have a project, we can click **Import from Git**. This will take us to a screen to authenticate against one of the Git platforms offered. If you're following along, that will be your GitHub account. Feel free to use any of the others, but we'll stick with GitHub.

Import an existing project from a Git repository

Connect your Git repo, push your code... and that's it! Or go back to choose a different deploy method.

Step 1 of 3

Connect to Git provider

Choose the Git provider where your site's source code is hosted. When you push to Git, we run your build tool of choice on our servers and deploy the result.

You can unlock options for self-hosted GitHub/GitLab by upgrading to the Business plan.

Figure 3.2 – A screenshot of the starting page for the import procedure
where you can choose where your project code is hosted

After you authenticate, Netlify will be able to display a list of repositories. From this list, select the repository we just created:

 netlify

Import an existing project from a Git repository

Connect your Git repo, push your code... and that's it! Or go back to choose a different deploy method.

Step 2 of 3

Pick a repository from GitHub

Choose the repository you want to link to your site on Netlify. When you push to Git, we run your build tool of choice on our servers and deploy the result.

🧑 brob ˅   🔍 eleventy

○ brob/11ty-landing-page   ›

○ brob/11ty-mixnmatch   ›

○ brob/11ty-second-11ty   ›

○ brob/11ty-serverless-color-converter   ›

○ brob/11ty-serverless-search   ›

○ brob/11ty.io   ›

Figure 3.3 – A screenshot of the view of the GitHub repository search built into Netlify

After a repository is chosen, Netlify will walk us through setting it up to deploy from its infrastructure. The main question Netlify has is which branch to deploy. If you follow GitHub's instructions, you should have a main branch. This is what we want to deploy:

 netlify

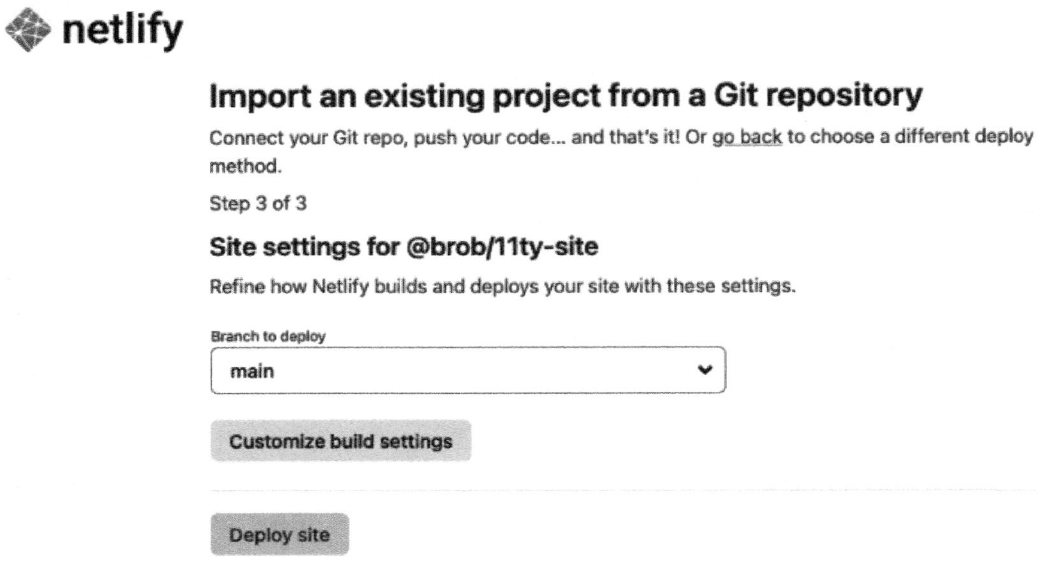

Import an existing project from a Git repository

Connect your Git repo, push your code... and that's it! Or go back to choose a different deploy method.

Step 3 of 3

Site settings for @brob/11ty-site

Refine how Netlify builds and deploys your site with these settings.

Branch to deploy

main	⌄

Customize build settings

Deploy site

Figure 3.4 – After selecting a repository, the basic build settings are required. In this screenshot, the project will use the main branch of the repository

Technically, this is all Netlify needs. That's because it can infer from our `package.json` what we want it to do. For the sake of clarity, however, click **Customize build settings**. This will display three more fields, two of which are already populated:

- **Base directory** tells Netlify which directory in the GitHub repository to choose to build from. If you didn't move your project to its own repository, this would be where you could choose which directory in the repository to build from. This is often referred to as monorepo support or building multiple sites from one repository.

- **Build command** lets Netlify know what terminal command to run. In our case, it saw our build command in the `package.json` file and populated it with `npm run build`, which is what we want.

- **Publish directory** is how Netlify knows where the final HTML will be stored after the build process. For default 11ty configurations, this will be `_site`.

Code-based configuration with netlify.toml

As an introduction to Netlify, the project dashboard is the easiest way to get started, however, you might want to automate this process more in the future. For that, you can specify these same variables with a file called `netlify.toml`. Any project with this file can automatically have these options applied when Netlify reads the source from GitHub. You can create the file manually or with the Netlify CLI. Both are nice options for power users:

- CLI: `https://docs.netlify.com/cli/get-started/`
- Netlify TOML: `https://docs.netlify.com/configure-builds/file-based-configuration/`

Once those fields are completed, click the **Deploy** button. That will take you to a newly created dashboard for the site with a deployment already running.

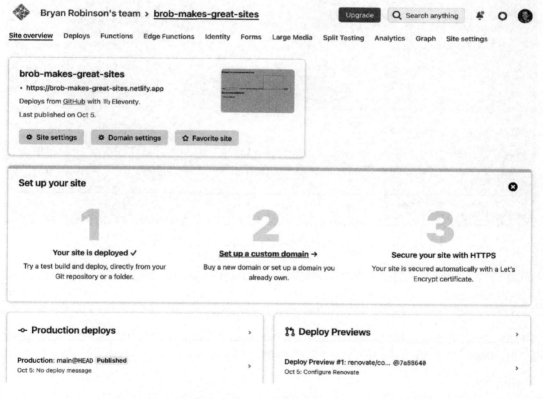

Figure 3.5 – Once the build configuration is set up, Netlify will direct you to the dashboard for the new project

Click the **Production build** link at the top and a deploy log will be shown. Our site is so small that by the time you find and click that link, it may already be done building. If at any point your site doesn't update, the deploy logs are where errors will be logged for debugging.

Figure 3.6 – An example log from the build process in the new project

Once the deployment is done, Netlify will provide you with a subdomain your project will live in. This can be changed in the project's site settings but has to be unique to any other sites deployed on its servers. Netlify also has the ability to point custom domains to sites hosted on its platform.

Custom domains can be found in your team settings. You can purchase them through Netlify or bring your own and point your domain's name servers to Netlify's servers.

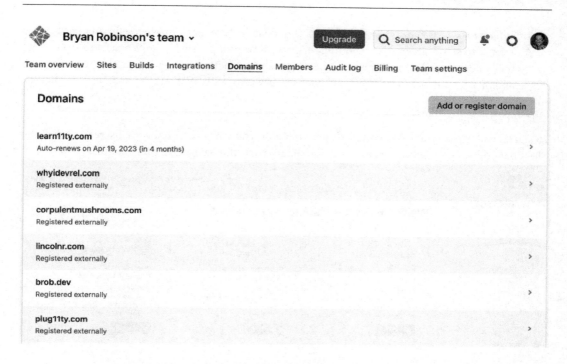

Figure 3.7 – The team settings page displaying all domains for the team

Now for the magic! How do you redeploy your site after making a change?

Make a change to any of the files in your project such as a page or a data file. Commit that change to Git and push the change up to GitHub. As soon as a new change is in the `main` branch on GitHub, Netlify will be notified and will automatically rebuild the site based on that new change. Once Netlify's build process is done, the changes will be live at the project's URL.

Most static site hosts will follow a similar pattern to Netlify. Let's take a look at another: **Cloudflare Pages**.

Deploying to Cloudflare Pages

Cloudflare is an older platform in terms of technology start-ups. Founded in 2010, its focus was primarily to act as a reverse proxy and CDN for websites. In late 2021, they entered the Jamstack space officially with the launch of their **Pages** product. Let's answer our hosting questions for Cloudflare Pages:

- *How will Cloudflare build pages?* Cloudflare has a full build pipeline that is able to utilize Node.js and npm packages such as 11ty.

- *How does Cloudflare serve pages?* Cloudflare's early offerings were specifically around CDNs. Cloudflare Pages uses the Cloudflare CDN to serve files.

- *What other services does Cloudflare offer?* Cloudflare's platform has more to offer than just things related to static site needs, including security, networking, privacy, and more. For static sites, they offer serverless functions with their Workers product, environment variable control, video and image on-demand services, and database services via R2, Workers KV, and Durable Objects.

Let's deploy to Cloudflare.

To start, create an account. When you're able to log in, you'll be presented with a screen and all the Cloudflare options. To set up a static site, click **Pages** from the navigation on the left.

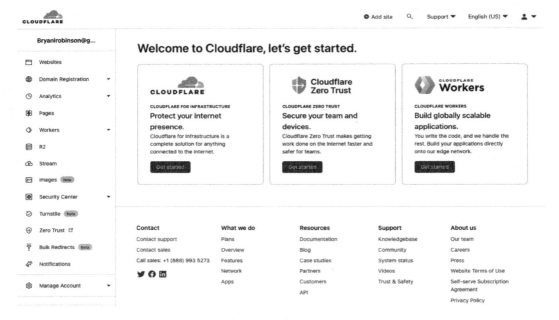

Figure 3.8 – Cloudflare's dashboard page after logging in

Much like Netlify, you'll be prompted to connect to a Git service. Again, select GitHub—like Netlify, there's an upload option here, as well.

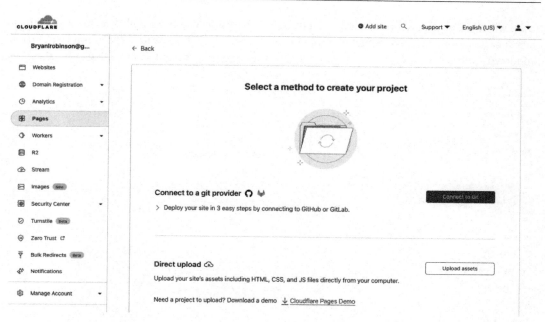

Figure 3.9 – A screenshot of the new Pages project page. From here,
you can select to upload or connect a Git provider

Once GitHub is connected, choose a repository from the list:

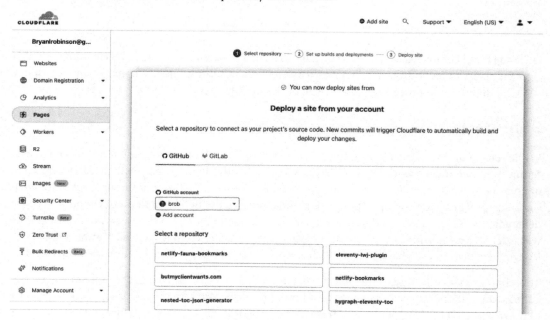

Figure 3.10 – Cloudflare's GitHub repository search page

This is where the platforms diverge a little. Cloudflare Pages does not detect our build needs. You can either enter your build command and output directory in the fields or select **Eleventy** from the **Framework** preset dropdown. Once selected, Cloudflare Pages' builders will begin working and show the log immediately.

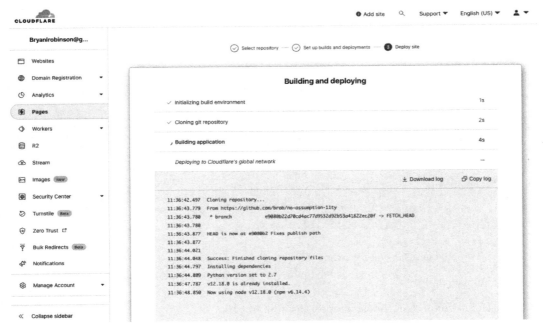

Figure 3.11 – Cloudflare's deploy build log

Once the build completes, your site will be available at a subdomain provided by Cloudflare. It also gives the ability to set up custom domains. To update the site, push an update to the GitHub repository and Cloudflare's build process will do the rest of the work for you.

Summary

While setting up 11ty via FTP or drag-and-drop is possible, it's often not ideal. For long-term use, setting up an automated workflow via GitHub and a host with a build pipeline will save large amounts of time and frustration. In this chapter, we covered questions to ask of your hosting providers for ideal static site processes, setting up 11ty via drag-and-drop, Netlify deployments, and Cloudflare Pages deployments. Netlify and Cloudflare are two trusted static site hosts, but there are others available as well, such as Vercel, Amazon Web Services, Microsoft Azure, and Google Cloud Platform. Each has its own benefits and drawbacks. Pick the service that best matches your needs and the needs of 11ty.

This chapter marks the end of the first project of the book. We set up a basic website in *Chapter 1*, added data to it in *Chapter 2*, and have now hosted it in *Chapter 3*. In the next chapter, we'll create a new project to build a blog with 11ty. This will build on the skills we learned during the project and we'll learn new skills around 11ty collections.

4

Building a Blog with Collections

In the first few chapters of this book, we set up a simple website. The pages had similar layouts and needs. To launch that site, we were able to work with just the very core functionality of 11ty and not extend it too much. In this chapter and *Chapter 5*, we'll be pushing 11ty further in order to create a blog site.

In this chapter, we'll set up the basic blog functionality using the concept of collections in 11ty, set up a special template for blog posts, work through date issues, and work with 11ty's concept of pagination to create a classic, minimal blog site.

We'll cover the following topics in the chapter:

- What is a collection?
- Creating a collection with directory data and Markdown
- Creating a custom template for blog posts
- Creating a paginated list of blog posts
- Creating dynamic category pages

Technical requirements

This is the beginning of project 2. In order to follow along, fork and clone the book's GitHub repository at `https://github.com/PacktPublishing/Eleventy-by-Example` and begin in `project-2/chapter-4/start`. The starting point for this project is a very basic 11ty site and can operate as a reminder of and practice for the basic project setup we covered in *Chapter 1*.

In this project, we'll start with an index page, a posts page, and a basic base layout. This project also uses Tailwind CSS for styling with Tailwind's CDN.

> **What is Tailwind CSS?**
>
> Tailwind is a "utility-first" CSS framework. We'll use this throughout the rest of the book for simple styling without needing to dive into the inner workings of CSS. Throughout the code examples, there will be various class names added to the HTML. These classes are how Tailwind will style the content.
>
> None of these classes is necessary to make the projects work, but they provide a nice finished product. Using the HTML without these classes will also work, and you can then apply your own styles if you wish.
>
> More information on Tailwind's CSS philosophy can be found here: `https://tailwindcss.com/`

What is a collection?

A collection is a special grouping of content inside of 11ty. At its core, a collection is created by a group of pages that have been associated with one another via the use of a `tags` array in a data cascade or via one of a few programmatic ways in the 11ty configuration.

By creating this grouping, a series of pages can be used as iterable data in any template via the 11ty `collections` object or manipulated into new combinations with 11ty's Collection API in the configuration file. Everything from blog posts and images to podcast episodes is better served through a collection instead of singular, unconnected pages.

With that definition in mind, let's create our first collection.

Creating a collection with directory data and Markdown

To start, let's create a new directory in our `src` folder named `posts`. This will be the directory that houses all the blog posts for our blog. Once that directory is created, add two Markdown files to the directory. The names of these files will, by default, be the URL for each post, so name them accordingly. For my posts, I'll use `my-first-blog-post.md` and `my-second-blog-post.md` – creative, I know.

Inside these files, we need a little bit of frontmatter and then the content written in Markdown. All Markdown is acceptable, but keep in mind the template we'll create will already have an `<h1>`, so it's best not to have one in the content for SEO and accessibility reasons:

```
---
title: My First Blog Post
layout: "layouts/base.html"
tags:
    - "post"
---
```

```
## This is a headline for a blog post

This is a paragraph for a blog post.
```

This creates a singular page and adds it to collections based on the tags listed in the `tags` array. The name and key for the collection are based on the string in the array.

Figure 4.1 – Output from the Markdown file

> **Warning: Tags**
>
> While it might be tempting to use the `tags` array for multiple use cases, resist that urge. The word "tags" has many connotations, including a way of categorizing content in blogs. While it is data that can be repurposed, the idea of tags in 11ty is specific to collections. If you use them for other purposes, it can create side effects in your project. Later in this chapter, we'll cover creating dynamic categories.

Now that we have two blog posts, we can use a collection, but before we do that, let's clean up the repeating data in these pages by using a directory data file.

Creating directory data for use in each post

If you recall from *Chapter 2*, you can create a JSON or JavaScript file with a specific name to add data to all pages within a directory. While it may seem for the two pieces of shared data that we'll want a simple JSON data file to share them, later in this chapter, we'll need a little dynamic JavaScript, so let's create a JavaScript directory data file. To do this, create a file in the `posts` directory named `posts.11tydata.js`. The `11tydata` in the filename is important for 11ty to recognize this as a data file and not a standard JavaScript file:

```
module.exports = {
    layout: "layouts/base.html",
    tags: ["post"],
    author: "Bryan Robinson"
}
```

In this file, we export an object that contains the data that we need. We know each blog post needs a layout and the `tags` array, but while we're here, why not add an author string with your name? This can be overridden in the frontmatter for each post, so having it for all posts means we can add a byline to each post without having to worry about conditionals later. Once this data file exists, we can remove the layout and tags data from each page's frontmatter. This makes creating blog posts much easier.

Now that we have unique data, we can set up a unique template for the posts.

Creating a custom template for blog posts

Figure 4.2 – Final blog post layout

We could continue to use the base template for our site on the blog posts, but we now have unique data for each page. We could set up conditionals on the base template to handle these, but if we want to create something starkly different from the base layout, it would become a mess of nested `if` statements.

To set up a new layout, create a new file in the `src/_templates/layouts` directory named `post.html`. From there, we need to refactor our base layout to use includes for the standard HTML. This will allow their reuse in the post layout.

Refer back to *Chapter 1* and try to set this up on your own as a challenge.

If you're not ready for that, we need to create `header.html` and `footer.html` files in the `/src/_templates/includes` directory. The header file will contain everything from the `Doctype` to the main `div` element that will contain the content of each page:

```
<!DOCTYPE html>
<html lang="en">
  <head>
    <meta charset="UTF-8" />
    <meta http-equiv="X-UA-Compatible" content="IE=edge" />
```

```html
    <meta name="viewport" content="width=device-width,
      initial-scale=1.0" />
    <title>My Blog Template</title>
    <!-- Bring your own CSS framework if you'd like -->
    <script src="https://cdn.tailwindcss.com?plugins=
      typography"></script>

</head>
<body class="bg-gray-100 font-sans leading-normal
  tracking-normal">
  <nav id="header" class="fixed w-full z--10 top-0">
    <div
      class="w-full md:max-w-4xl mx-auto flex flex-wrap
        items-center justify-between mt-0 py-3"
    >
      <div class="pl-4">
        <a
          class="text-gray-900 no-underline
            hover:no-underline font-extrabold text-xl"
          href="#"
        >
          My Blog
        </a>
      </div>
      <div
      class="lg:flex lg:items-center lg:w-auto
        bg-gray-100 md:bg-transparent z--20"
      id="nav-content"
      >
      <ul class="list-reset lg:flex justify-end
        flex-1 items-center">
        <li class="mr-3">
          <a class="inline-block py-2 px-4
            text-gray-900" href="/posts">
            Posts
          </a>
        </li>
      </ul>
    </div>
  </div>

  </nav>
  <div class="container max-w-3xl px-4
    mx-auto pt-20 prose">
```

The `footer` include will close that `body` div and then close the `body` and `html` elements:

```
    </footer>
</body>
</html>
```

Once these files are in place, open the base layout – `src/_templates/layouts/base.html` – and replace the HTML in those areas with includes:

```
{% include 'includes/header.html' %}

{% if title %}<h1>{{ title }}</h1>{% endif %}

{{ content }}

{% include 'includes/footer.html' %}
```

From there, we can create the main elements for the blog post template. While we could create a drastically different layout now, let's focus on small changes that will make sense for a post page. We can add the byline and adjust the margins on the headline and byline to tie them tightly together visually:

```
{% include 'includes/header.html' %}

{% if title %}<h1 class="mb-1">{{ title }}</h1>{% endif %}

{% if author %}<p class="m-0">By {{ author }} |
  Posted on {{ dateString }}</p>{% endif %}


{{ content }}

{% include 'includes/footer.html' %}
```

When the new layout is saved, the data for our posts can be updated to use the new layout:

```
module.exports = {
    layout: "layouts/post.html",
    tags: ["post"],
    author: "Bryan Robinson",
}
```

My First Blog Post

By Bryan Robinson

This is a headline for a blog post

This is a paragraph for a blog post.

Figure 4.3 – Result of adding the new layout

This change will trickle down to all pages in this directory. We're almost done with the basics, but one more important piece of data is required for proper blog listing and display: a date.

Adding content dates to blog posts

By default, 11ty creates a date for each page that gets added. This date can be accessed using the `page.date` variable. The problem with this for blog posts is that that date will be created when the page is built – meaning when the site is built in our host, whatever day that happens to be is what the `page.date` variable will store. That's not ideal for blog posts that may have been written days or years before.

Beyond the creation date, 11ty allows dates to be added to pages in a couple of different ways:

- **Filename**: If a date string is added to the beginning of a filename, 11ty will strip it from the final URL and use it as the content's date. For example, a file named `2022-01-01-my-slug-here.md` will have a final URL of `my-slug-here` and a date of January 1st, 2022. If you're migrating from platforms such as Jekyll, this will seem familiar.

- **Variables in data**: If a `date` key is added to the data cascade for a particular page, it will be available for the page's date.

While I originally started my static site journey in Jekyll, I find that adding the `date` value in frontmatter or data files allows the most flexibility, so that's the direction we'll use here.

The `date` variable allows multiple value types. It has a series of keywords that provide automatic functionality, such as `Last modified Created`, `git Last Modified`, or `git Created`, but getting a specific date will always be best for content such as blog posts. To set an explicit date, add it as a valid YAML date value or ISO 8601 string.

To the frontmatter of our blog posts, let's add a `date` variable:

```
---
title: My First Blog Post
date: "2022-01-01"
---
```

Once the posts are updated, we can add `page.date` to our `posts` template to display the date the post was published:

```
{% include 'includes/header.html' %}
{% if title %}<h1 class="mb-1">{{ title }}</h1>{% endif %}

<p class="m-0">By {{ author }} | Posted on
  {{ page.date }}</p>

{{ content }}

{% include 'includes/footer.html' %}
```

This will output a JavaScript date string to our HTML. Depending on your timezone – or the timezone of your host – you may notice a problem. I added January 1st to my data, but my site is displaying December 31st. That's because 11ty stores the date as UTC time at midnight of the date. Depending on the build environment and timezone, this could display the previous day. This inconsistency is a problem and is listed on the 11ty website as a common pitfall (`https://www.11ty.dev/docs/dates/#dates-off-by-one-day`). The 11ty documentation suggests either using Nunjucks for a template language to allow our template to run JavaScript or creating a Liquid filter to change the date. I'd like to suggest a third way: use the directory data file to create a new date string for each post based on the page date.

11ty already ships with the Luxon JavaScript date package for working with dates (`https://github.com/moment/luxon`), so we can use that within our `posts` JavaScript data file to manipulate the date and output the exact string format we'd like as a new variable on each page.

There's one new feature we need to use to work with the current page information: 11ty's computed data. The computed data is data added as the last step in 11ty's Data Cascade. It can be used along the cascade but injects the data at the very end. This means we have all the data available when this runs. This allows us to take each page's date and convert it into a directory data file. We don't have this functionality as a regular element of the file; we need it to live under a specific key in the object we output from the JavaScript data file: `eleventyComputed`.

The `eleventyComputed` object accepts functions as its properties. Each function has the whole scope of 11ty data as a potential argument and will inject the data returned as an item in the page's `data` object (where things such as frontmatter data are stored). In our use case, we don't need the entire data object; instead, we just want to destructure the `page`-specific data from it. From there, we can run specific functions from the Luxon date library to set the date's time zone and output a string using one of Luxon's predefined patterns for dates:

```
const { DateTime } = require("luxon")
module.exports = {
    layout: "layouts/post.html",
    tags: ["post"],
```

```
    author: "Bryan Robinson",
    eleventyComputed: {
        dateString: ({page}) => DateTime.fromJSDate
        (page.date, {zone: 'utc'}).toLocaleString
            (DateTime.DATE_FULL)
    }
}
```

Now instead of using `page.date` where we need the date, we use the newly created `dateString` variable. This is tied to the page's date but outputs a specific string value always from the UTC time for consistency:

```
{% include 'includes/header.html' %}
{% if title %}<h1 class="mb-1">{{ title }}</h1>{% endif %}

<p class="m-0">By {{ author }} | Posted on
  {{ dateString }}</p>

{{ content }}

{% include 'includes/footer.html' %}
```

Once the code is updated, we should have a date in the output.

My First Blog Post

By Bryan Robinson | Posted on January 1, 2021

This is a headline for a blog post

This is a paragraph for a blog post.

Figure 4.4 – Output after adding the date

Now that the dates are taken care of, let's add one more feature to our post template: a link to the next or previous blog post.

Displaying the next or previous blog post

From my days as a user experience professional making news websites and then marketing websites for clients, one of the important edicts I followed was, "Always give the user a next step." To that end, once a user is done reading one of our blog posts, wouldn't it be nice to let them know what the next post is?

While that may seem like a big undertaking, 11ty has some built-in collection functionality to help us get this done. 11ty has a built-in filter that can accept a collection and return the next or previous page in that collection.

At the bottom of the post layout, add the following code:

```
<!-- create nextPost and previousPost variables -->
<!-- Set the variables to the next and previous items on the
collections.post Collection -->
{% assign nextPost = collections.post |
    getNextCollectionItem%}
{% assign previousPost = collections.post |
    getPreviousCollectionItem%}

{% if nextPost %}
    <div class="mt-4">
        <h3>Next Post</h3>
        <h4><a href="{{ nextPost.url }}">
            {{ nextPost.data.title }}</a></h4>
    </div>
{% endif %}
{% if previousPost %}
    <div class="mt-4">
        <h3>Previous Post</h3>
        <h4><a href="{{ previousPost.url }}">
            {{ previousPost.data.title }}</a></h4>
    </div>
{% endif %}
```

This will display the previous post and the next post at the bottom of each post, if one exists – no complex logic or JavaScript necessary:

Figure 4.5 – Output of the next- and previous-post code

Now that we have a post template squared away with dates and additional features, let's create a list page so that users can navigate to our pages.

Creating a paginated list of blog posts

For our blog, we want a nice list of posts on the `/posts/` route. Luckily, the start of this project already has the `posts.html` page. We just need to adjust it to loop through the collection we just made and create links to each post that will entice a user to read one.

Figure 4.6 – Paginated pages finished

To do that, we'll use a `for` loop, as we did for the triptychs in *Chapter 2*, but this time we'll use the collections array that's provided by 11ty:

```
---
title: "All Posts"
layout: 'layouts/base.html'
---
{% for post in collections.post %}
    <article>
        <h2 class="mb-1">
            <a href="{{ post.url }}">{{ post.data.title }}
                </a>
        </h2>
        <p>By {{ post.data.author }} | Posted on
            {{ post.data.dateString }}</p>
    </article>
{% endfor %}
```

To access the collection, we reference the array with the `collections` key and the name of the tag used in the post data. When looping through it, anything available on the `page` object will be accessible via the `post` variable. The frontmatter and additional data for the post will be available at `post.data`. So, to access the title, we need `post.data.title`, but to access the URL for the page, it can be accessed with `post.url`.

This is a nice start, but many blogs also contain a description for each item. It helps readers understand what they're about to read. To add this to our blog, add a `description` variable to each blog post. Using the > symbol in the description allows multi-line text and a better editing experience for longer-form content:

```
---
title: My First Blog Post
description: >
    This is a description of my first blog post.
    It's a little short, but that's okay.
date: "2021-01-01"
---
```

Once each blog post has a description, let's add it to the post listing. Just in case a post doesn't have one, let's make sure to put a conditional around it:

```
{% for post in collections.post %}
    <article>
        <h2 class="mb-1">
            <a href="{{ post.url }}">{{ post.data.title }}
                </a>
        </h2>
        <p>By {{ post.data.author }} | Posted on
            {{ post.data.dateString }}</p>

        {% if post.data.description %}
            <p>{{ post.data.description }}</p>
        {% endif %}
    </article>
{% endfor %}
```

We now have a compelling list of blog posts. The order of them is problematic. The oldest blog posts are first. This is the default date ordering, but blogs are typically ordered in reverse chronological order. While we could use Liquid's reverse filter to change this, that would mutate the data every time it's called and have odd side effects. Instead, we can change the order in the 11ty configuration file.

To do this, we can use the 11ty Collection API to get this specific collection and reverse the array in the `eleventy.config.js` configuration file. This makes for consistent usage in every template and means there is no need to worry about side effects:

```
module.exports = function(eleventyConfig) {
    // Set the collection to reverse chronological order
    eleventyConfig.addCollection("post", (collection) => {
        return collection.getFilteredByTag
            ("post").reverse();
    });
    // ... The rest of the configuration file
```

In this code, we use the `addCollection` method to add a collection named `post`. The second argument of `add collection` is a function used to create the collection. It is passed the `collection` API object.

There are multiple ways of accessing collections – getting all collection items and filtering, filtering based on folder structure and glob – but for our use, we'll get all the collection items filtered by a tag string: `post`.

Once we have that, we call the JavaScript `reverse()` array method and can return that new array back. This gives us a collection named `post` – which we're already using – and it contains all the items tagged `post` in reverse chronological order.

For our two-post blog, this is enough, but what happens when we have 100 posts? That would be too many for one page. We need to paginate these posts on our list page.

Paginating the list page

11ty has pagination functionality built in. It can sometimes feel overwhelming but offers a lot of flexibility in how it can be used. In fact, in *Chapter 9*, we'll use pagination to create pages from a headless CMS. With great power comes great complexity.

To start, we need to modify the `posts.html` page with additional frontmatter data. We'll use the `pagination` object in 11ty to describe how we want these pages built:

```
---
title: "All Posts"
layout: 'layouts/base.html'
pagination:
  data: collections.post
  size: 2
  alias: posts
---
```

The pagination object takes a data variable. This data can come from data files, frontmatter, or, in our case, the `collections.post` array. It also accepts a `size` variable. This is how many items per page to display. Let's set that to 2. The `alias` property is optional. It assigns the `pagination.items` array to a shorter, more readable variable. You don't have to use it, but saving typing means saving typos and bugs.

> **More content**
>
> Now's a great time to add more content. I'd recommend at least having 10 blog posts to test this out. It doesn't have to be real blog posts, but duplicating each post and changing its frontmatter and filename can go a long way to seeing pagination in action.

Now that we have the data, we need to modify the loop on the page to loop through the new paginated array instead of the full collection array. Each page in our pagination has two posts (or however many you assign with the `size` property). So, by changing the `for` tag from `collections.post` to the new alias of `posts`, we should see only two posts on the page instead of however many blog posts are currently on the site. As long as we keep the loop's key set to `post`, we won't have to make any changes to the content of the loop:

```
{% for post in posts %}
    <article>
        <h2 class="mb-1">
            <a href="{{ post.url }}">{{ post.data.title }}</a>
        </h2>
        <p>By {{ post.data.author }} | Posted on
            {{ post.data.dateString }}</p>

        {% if post.data.description %}
            <p>{{ post.data.description }}</p>
        {% endif %}
    </article>
{% endfor %}
```

Now we only have two posts listed! Experiment a little with pagination size and see how 11ty adapts this page. Once you're done with that, we need to find a way to access the rest of the pages.

If you pay attention to the terminal as 11ty runs, you can find the URLs for each page of our posts, but there's no visible link to them. Let's change that by creating next, previous, and page count items at the bottom of the page.

```
[11ty] Writing _site/posts/category/blog/index.html from ./src/category.html (liquid)
[11ty] Writing _site/index.html from ./src/index.html (liquid)
[11ty] Writing _site/posts/index.html from ./src/posts/posts.html (liquid)
[11ty] Writing _site/posts/my-third-post/index.html from ./src/posts/my-third-post.md (liquid)
[11ty] Writing _site/posts/category/personal/index.html from ./src/category.html (liquid)
[11ty] Writing _site/posts/my-second-blog-post/index.html from ./src/posts/my-second-blog-post.md
iquid)
[11ty] Writing _site/posts/my-first-blog-post/index.html from ./src/posts/my-first-blog-post.md
uid)
[11ty] Writing _site/posts/category/development/index.html from ./src/category.html (liquid)
[11ty] Writing _site/posts/1/index.html from ./src/posts/posts.html (liquid)
[11ty] Wrote 9 files in 0.12 seconds (v2.0.0)
```

Figure 4.7 – Terminal output for the pages created by 11ty

In the pagination data that 11ty provides, there are two useful items for making the pagination controls: the `href` object and the `hrefs` array.

The `href` object has URLs for first, last, next, and previous. We'll use next and previous for creating links to those pages. The `hrefs` array has a list of URLs in order for each page: perfect for creating anchors to each page.

To keep our main template cleaner, let's abstract the pagination out to its own include: `includes/pagination.html`.

In this file, we'll check whether there is a previous or next `href` item. If there is, we'll have a link on the page that appears active; if not, it will be a span that appears inactive. We will also loop through all the URLs in the `hrefs` array and link to them with display text equaling the counter (using Liquid's `forloop.index`):

```
<!-- If there's a previous href, have previous be a link -->
{% if pagination.href.previous %}
    <a href="{{ pagination.href.previous }}" class=
        "bg-blue-500 hover:bg-blue-700 text-white font-bold
            py-2 px-4 rounded">Previous</a>
{% else %}
    <span class="bg-gray-200 text-gray-500 font-bold py-2
        px-4 rounded">Previous</span>
{% endif %}

<!-- Loop through all hrefs and build out an anchor for each and the
page number (based on the loop counter) -->
{% for item in pagination.hrefs %}
    <a href="{{ item }}" class="bg-blue-500 hover:bg-blue-700 text-
white font-bold py-2 px-4 rounded">{{ forloop.index }}</a>
{% endfor %}

<!-- If there's a next href, have next be a link -->
{% if pagination.href.next %}
    <a href="{{ pagination.href.next }}" class="bg-blue-500
        hover:bg-blue-700 text-white font-bold py-2 px-4
            rounded">Next</a>
{% else %}
    <span class="bg-gray-200 text-gray-500 font-bold py-2
        px-4 rounded">Next</span>
{% endif %}
```

Then, we'll add this `include` to the `posts` page if the `hrefs` array has a length greater than 1 (if it's not greater than 1, pagination controls would be pointless):

```
{% if pagination.hrefs.length > 1 %}
    {% include "includes/pagination.html" %}
{% endif %}
```

Now, we have a fully functional blog. We still are missing an optional but fairly standard feature of most blogs: categories. In the next section, we'll create dynamic category pages using a plugin, pagination, and an array of categories on each blog post.

Creating dynamic category pages

Blogs have categories. Our blog should have categories. They're great for organization, user experience, and search engine optimization.

Blog entries with category "blog"

- <u>My Third Blog Post</u>

- <u>My First Blog Post</u>

Figure 4.8 – Blog category page

By default, 11ty doesn't have anything built-in for creating categories. This has led many people to try to use tags for categories with collections, but this ends up crossing purposes with tags and it's best left to a new piece of functionality. To do this succinctly, we'll use an 11ty plugin.

We'll cover plugins in depth in the second half of the book, but for now, know that plugins in 11ty are portable configurations that make anything you can do in the 11ty configuration portable to more projects. For our categorization needs, we'll use a plugin that can inspect all of the posts collection, find a categories array, and help us create a category pagination template to display all the posts – or paginated posts – for a category. This is possible without a plugin but requires a lot of JavaScript that is ancillary to 11ty.

> **Going deeper into the plugin**
>
> Want to dive deeper into the plugin? You can find out more with this YouTube walk-through: `https://www.youtube.com/watch?v=DC28C0sGG4w`.

To install the plugin, we need to install it as an NPM package:

```
npm install eleventy-plugin-dynamic-categories
```

Once it's installed, we can require it at the top of the `eleventy.config.js` file and add it to the project via the `addPlugin` method on the `eleventyConfig` object. There are multiple configuration options for the plugin, but the two we'll update are `categoryVar`, to tell the plugin what the category's variable name is, and `itemsCollection`, to tell the plugin what our collection is named:

```
const dynamicCategories = require('eleventy-plugin-dynamic-
categories');
module.exports = function(eleventyConfig) {
    // Set the collection to reverse chronological order
    eleventyConfig.addCollection("post", (collection) => {
```

```
            return collection.getFilteredByTag
                ("post").reverse();
    });
    eleventyConfig.addPlugin(dynamicCategories, {
        categoryVar: "categories", // Name of your category
      variable from your frontmatter (default: categories)
        itemsCollection: "post", // Name of your collection
            to use for the items (default: posts)
    })

    // ... The rest of the configuration
}
```

This plugin then gives us a couple of new collections that we can use for pagination. Before we build out our category pages, we need to add categories. To each of the blog posts, add a `categories` array in the frontmatter. Each category will be a string and should be formatted for viewing by users (the plugin handles making slugs out of the strings for use in URLs later):

```
---
title: My First Blog Post
description: >
    This is a description of my first blog post.
    It's a little short, but that's okay.
date: "2021-01-01"
categories:
    - "Development"
    - "11ty"
    - "JavaScript"
---
```

This gives us all the data we need to use the plugin and get a page built for each category. To build those pages, we need to use 11ty pagination again, this time against the new collection built by the plugin.

Create a new page in the `src` directory named `category.html`. This will be the template used for each category in the pagination. Just like before, we give the pagination object the data to use, an alias, and a size. This time, the size is `1`. We want one category page generated for each category in the collection.

It needs a layout as well. The base layout is fine for this page. Then, we need two new items. First is the `permalink` variable. This is a pattern for each page in pagination to use. This could have been used earlier in the previous pagination example, but the numeric permalinks were fine for that example. For categories, we want a special URL for each. To do that, we provide a string and can use a Liquid variable to get the `slug` of the individual category. The slug is a slugified version of the name for each category. For example, **My Category** would become **my-category**.

The second new item is the use of `eleventyComputed` in the frontmatter. As we covered earlier, 11ty's computed data is the last data added to the Data Cascade and can be used to compute specialized content based on all the data in the cascade. In this case, we want to make a custom title based on the category's title. After the frontmatter, we can loop through the posts in the category's `posts` array – again, generated by the plugin:

```
---
pagination:
    data: collections.categories
    alias: category
    size: 1
permalink: /posts/category/{{ category.slug }}/
layout: "layouts/base.html"
eleventyComputed:
    title: Posts in the "{{ category.title }}" category
---
<ul>
{% for post in category.posts %}
<li>
    <a href="{{ post.url }}">{{ post.data.title }}</a>
</li>
{% endfor %}
</ul>
```

For this template, we'll go more concise for the layout and just display a bulleted list of items. Each of these will link directly to the page as built in the `posts` directory. If you want to extend this further, you can also adjust the category template to take advantage of paginated posts in each category. This is a much more complex use case than typical pagination but can be done with the plugin's `categoriesByPage` collection and additional data. It doesn't use typical 11ty pagination for creating page numbers but comes with a helper shortcode for generating the markup for pagination navigation. In the following example, see the `{% pagination category %}` code for its use:

```
---
layout: layouts/base.html
# Default permalink scheme (still able to be customized)
permalink: /posts/category/{{category.permalinkScheme}}
pagination:
  data: collections.categoriesByPage
  size: 1
  alias: category
  addAllPagesToCollections: true
eleventyComputed:
  title: Blog entries with category &quot;{{ category.slug
    }}&quot;
---
```

```
{% for post in category.posts %}
<li>
    <a href="{{post.url}}">{{ post.data.title }}</a>
</li>
{% endfor %}

<!-- Helper function -->
{% pagination category %}
```

By default, each page will have five posts, and that can be adjusted by the plugin's `perPageCount` option:

```
eleventyConfig.addPlugin(dynamicCategories, {
    categoryVar: "categories", // Name of your category
    variable from your frontmatter (default: categories)
    itemsCollection: "post", // Name of your collection
        to use for the items (default: posts)
    perPageCount: 10 // Items per page of your
        paginated category (default: 5)
})
```

Whether you choose to implement the pagination on categories or just the default category pages, the first part of our blog is now done!

Summary

We now have a fully functioning blog with many of the features you'd expect. It can all be authored in Markdown inside of a GitHub repository and hosted in the same way we hosted project 1 in *Chapter 3*. In setting up the blog, we covered the functionality that comes with collections. We set up a custom template that used the special data in the new post collection. We then built a list page for all the blog posts and paginated it. We then used a specialized plugin to create dynamic category pages based on the arrays of categories listed on each blog post.

In the next chapter, we'll extend this further and work on adding different content types to the blog posts, including YouTube videos, CodePen embeds, and custom blockquote functionality.

Creating Custom Shortcodes to Add Mixed Media to Markdown

Now that we have a basic blog, let's make that blog stand out with various forms of media. The flavor of Markdown that 11ty uses allows for the use of HTML, so we could embed things like YouTube videos or CodePen pens with their basic HTML embeds, but that can be a lot of repetitive markup that needs to be added and modified on each blog post. Custom shortcodes allow us to set a standard template for each of these types of media and use a simplified tag in the Markdown files of our blog posts (and in any of our templates, as well).

In this chapter, we'll cover the following basics of 11ty's shortcodes and set up three different shortcodes to make our blog posts more fully featured:

- What is a shortcode?
- Creating a YouTube embed
- Creating a custom blockquote with semantic HTML
- Creating a CodePen embed with a customizable display

By the end of this chapter, we'll have a fully-functioning developer blog with three customized shortcodes for use in our Markdown files.

Technical requirements

This is the second chapter of the second project. If you followed along with *Chapter 4*, use the project you've already been working on. If you didn't write code for *Chapter 4*, use the book's GitHub repository at `https://github.com/PacktPublishing/Eleventy-by-Example` and use `project-2/chapter-5/start`.

What is a shortcode?

Believe it or not, you've already been using shortcodes in this book. The template tags we've used to do things such as loops and conditionals are shortcodes. In their template engines, they're usually referred to as "tags." In the case of 11ty, the custom shortcode functionality is used as a wrapper and set of conveniences around each template engine's custom tag functionality.

This allows 11ty developers to develop tags for individual languages or all the template languages and use the same syntax.

Not all template engines support custom shortcodes. According to the 11ty documentation, the engines that support shortcodes are Liquid, Nunjucks, Handlebars, and JavaScript templates. While the basic functionality is universal, each template engine has its own unique features, as well.

> ### Keyword arguments
>
> One example of differences is the use of keyword arguments inside of Nunjucks. 11ty's Nunjucks implementation supports named keyword arguments, whereas the Liquid implementation does not. While this does not significantly affect the use of shortcodes, the keyword arguments in Nunjucks can make complex shortcodes a little easier to handle.

```
// Liquid
{% myTag "first-arg" "second argument" "third argument" %}
// Nunjucks with keyword arguments
{% myTag "first-arg", {second="second argument",
    third="third argument"} %}
```

In this chapter, we'll focus on making what 11ty considers "universal" shortcodes. These shortcodes will work in the template engines listed above. Each engine has different ways of calling the shortcode in templates:

```
// Liquid (optional comma between arguments)
{% myTag "first" "second" %}
// Nunjucks (comma required)
{% myTag "first", second" %}
// Handlebars (Using triple braces)
{{{ myTag "first" "second" }}}
// JavaScript (used as a function)
${this.myTag("first", "second")}
```

By default, 11ty's Markdown rendering happens in Liquid. What this means is that any shortcode available in Liquid will be available in our blog posts, as well as any other Liquid templates. The default rendering engine for Markdown can be changed. If it's changed in the configuration, then that engine will be used to render — for example, setting the Markdown renderer to Handlebars would mean changing the syntax from {% %} to {{{ }}} for each shortcode.

Let's dive into creating our first shortcode: a YouTube embed.

Creating a YouTube embed

While YouTube provides a basic HTML embed when you click **Share** on its site, making it responsive — able to work at various screen sizes and on various devices — requires a little bit of extra work. This extra work would be necessary every single time you want to add a new YouTube video to your blog. Extra work is not what we want when writing. In this case, we can make a shortcode to do that work for us.

Getting the correct markup for a YouTube embed

To start, go to any YouTube video and click the **Share** button below it and then click **Embed**. This will pop up a window with a few options and the code needed: an iframe.

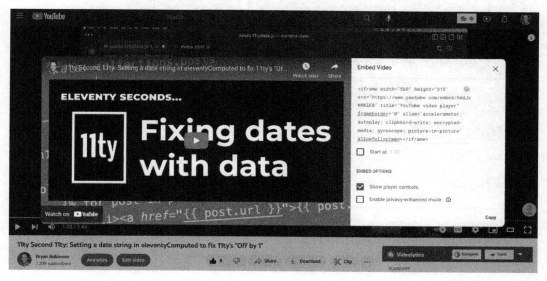

Figure 5.1 – The YouTube embed screen showing the options for creating an embed and the code needed

Feel free to use the following code, as it's formatted more nicely than what YouTube will give you. Add this code to any of your blog post files:

```
<iframe
    width="560"
    height="315"
    src="https://www.youtube.com/embed/VddJxNKKlE8"
    title="YouTube video player"
    frameborder="0"
    allow="accelerometer; autoplay; clipboard-write;
        encrypted-media; gyroscope; picture-in-picture"
    allowfullscreen></iframe>
```

Putting this code in your Markdown will generate the YouTube player.

This is a paragraph for a blog post.This is a paragraph for a blog post.This is a paragraph for a blog post.This is a paragraph for a blog post.

This is a paragraph for a blog post.This is a paragraph for a blog post.This is a paragraph for a blog post.This is a paragraph for a blog post.

Figure 5.2 – The YouTube player embedded in the blog post

While this works by default, it doesn't scale up or down — it's not responsive. While that was fine a decade ago, again, this is no longer something that is accepted on most sites.

This is a paragraph for a blog post.This is a paragraph for a blog post.This is a paragraph for a blog post.This is a paragraph for a blog post.

This is a paragraph for a blog post.This is a paragraph for a blog post.This is a paragraph for a blog post.This is a paragraph for a blog post.

Figure 5.3 – The screen size of the blog has been reduced, but the YouTube player stays the same size – not ideal for responsive design

Let's alter the HTML generated with some modern CSS to make the embed full width and keep its aspect ratio as it shrinks.

Modern CSS

For this example, we'll use the new `aspect-ratio` CSS property. This has full support in all modern browsers, but it should be noted that the browser support for this property is at about 91% of global users according to caniuse.com at the time of this writing. That said, this solution is much more elegant than the former "CSS hack" that required multiple containers and absolute positioning. If you need to support browsers such as Internet Explorer, look up Chris Coyier's responsive video tutorial on CSS Tricks: `https://css-tricks.com/fluid-width-video/`

By removing the set height and width and using the `aspect-ratio` property and a width of 100%, we can force the video to scale at the proper rate for most YouTube videos:

```
<iframe
    style="aspect-ratio: 16 / 9; width: 100%"
    src="https://www.youtube.com/embed/VddJxNKKlE8"
    title="YouTube video player"
    frameborder="0"
    allow="accelerometer; autoplay; clipboard-write;
        encrypted-media; gyroscope; picture-in-picture"
    allowfullscreen></iframe>
```

Now, the video will scale all the way up and be responsive to the screen size all the way down to mobile.

Figure 5.4 – The old and new video players showcasing how the new video player fills the width of the blog post column

To do this on every video we ever put on our site would be tedious. Let's refactor this into a custom shortcode. To make it as easy as possible, we'll have the shortcode accept the video's ID, which can be copied from any YouTube URL, and an optional title — not the title in the HTML provided by YouTube, which is helpful for SEO and accessibility.

Setting up the shortcode

Shortcodes are defined in the 11ty configuration file: `eleventy.config.js`.

> **Changes to the configuration**
>
> Changes to the configuration file will require restarting 11ty. As you add new things to the file, be sure to *ctrl+c* in your terminal window and rerun `npm run dev` to see the latest changes.

The `addShortcode` method accepts a string as its first argument. This string will be what the shortcode is called in our templates. The second argument is the function used to create a string to return. If the shortcode doesn't return anything, 11ty will throw an error. Before we add our shortcode, the `eleventy.config.js` file should look like the following code:

```
const dynamicCategories = require
    ('eleventy-plugin-dynamic-categories');

module.exports = function(eleventyConfig) {
    // We'll add our shortcode here

    eleventyConfig.addCollection("post", (collection) => {

        return collection.getFilteredByTag
            ("post").reverse();

    });

    eleventyConfig.addPlugin(dynamicCategories, {

        categoryVar: "categories", // Name of your category
        variable from your frontmatter (default: categories)

        itemsCollection: "post",
// Name of your collection to use for the items (default: posts)

        perPageCount: 10
    // Items per page of your paginated category (default: 5)

    })
```

```
// Copy `assets/` to `_site/assets/`

eleventyConfig.addPassthroughCopy("assets");



// Set the source for 11ty to the /src directory

// Otherwise, this defaults to the project root

// This provides a cleaner project structure

return {

    dir: {

        input: "src",

        output: "_site",
// This is the default, but it's included here for clarity.

        includes: "_templates"

    }

  }

}
```

We'll then add the following code to the function that's exported from the file:

```
eleventyConfig.addShortcode("youtube", () => {
    return `<iframe
        style="aspect-ratio: 16 / 9; width: 100%"
        src="https://www.youtube.com/embed/VddJxNKKlE8"
        title="YouTube video player"
        frameborder="0"
        allow="accelerometer; autoplay; clipboard-
            write; encrypted-media; gyroscope;
                picture-in-picture"
        allowfullscreen></iframe>`
})
```

This shortcode can now be used in any template of Markdown:

```
{% youtube %}
```

This will always render that singular video. That's not ideal for what we need. Let's make it dynamically build based on the two arguments we mentioned before.

The new syntax for the shortcode should have the ID and an optional title:

```
{% youtube "VddJxNKKlE8", "This my title" %}
```

Then we can add those two strings as arguments in the function for our shortcode and use that data in the template literal we return. To make the title optional, be sure to add a default value for `title` in the function initialization:

```
eleventyConfig.addShortcode("youtube",
    (id, title="A YouTube Video") => {
    return `<iframe
        style="aspect-ratio: 16 / 9; width: 100%"
        src="https://www.youtube.com/embed/${id}"
        title="${title}"
        frameborder="0"
        allow="accelerometer; autoplay;
            clipboard-write; encrypted-media;
                gyroscope; picture-in-picture"
        allowfullscreen></iframe>`
})
```

With that, you have a shortcode that can be used in any template or Markdown to embed a YouTube video based on the ID provided by the YouTube URL and is fully responsive and ready for any container that it gets added to.

Next, let's extend the base functionality of Markdown with a new, more robust blockquote.

Creating a custom blockquote with semantic HTML

The basic Markdown syntax allows for blockquotes, but it doesn't allow for citations in blockquotes. Let's add that functionality to our site with a shortcode. While we could use a regular shortcode with the quotation inside an argument, the developer experience of that is a little lacking. In this case, we can use an 11ty **paired shortcode**. A paired shortcode is a shortcode that has an opening tag and a closing tag, much like the standard conditional or `for` loop in Liquid.

Creating the proper semantic HTML for a block quote

Let's start with the proper HTML for a blockquote. According to MDN, a block quote should be inside a figure with a `figcaption` to describe the author and the cited media source, which should reside within a `cite` tag:

> *"It's worth noting that the W3C specification says that a reference to a creative work, as included within a <cite> element, may include the name of the work's author. However, the WHATWG specification for <cite> says the opposite: that a person's name must never be included, under any circumstances." (https:// developer.mozilla.org/en-US/docs/Web/HTML/Element/cite)*

We'll go with their definitions for proper semantic quotes. To that end, the HTML should look like the following:

```
<figure class="blockquote">
  <blockquote>
    <p>This is a blockquote for a blog post.</p>
  </blockquote>
  <figcaption class="blockquote cite">
    By Bryan Robinson in <cite>https://bryanlrobinson.com
      </cite>
  </figcaption>
</figure>
```

This is quite a bit more HTML than what is provided by the standard Markdown blockquote:

```
<blockquote>
    <p>This is a paragraph for a blog post. This is a
       paragraph for a blog post.This is a paragraph for a
         blog post.This is a paragraph for a blog post.</p>
</blockquote>
```

This time, let's define our shortcode syntax first and work backwards into the configuration code. We need the content of the quotation, an author, and a work to cite. The content should go between our shortcode tags to allow for maximum readability:

```
{% blockquote "Bryan Robinson" "https://bryanlrobinson.com"
   %}
This is a **blockquote** for a blog post.
{% endblockquote %}
```

The author and the citation can be added in the same argument syntax that we used for the YouTube player, but now we have a large amount of space that allows for additional creation. It would also be good to be able to use Markdown syntax in the tag to keep the editing power the same as the rest of the page.

Let's set this up in our configuration file.

Setting up the shortcode

In the `eleventy.config.js` configuration file, we'll add a new element to the function the file exports. This time instead of the `addShortcode` method, we'll use the `addPairedShortcode` method. The main difference between these methods is that the first argument of the creation function will be the content that is between the paired shortcode tags:

```
eleventyConfig.addPairedShortcode("blockquote",
    (content, author, cite) => {
    const markup = `
    <figure class="blockquote">
        <blockquote>
            ${content}
        </blockquote>
        <figcaption class="blockquote cite">
            By ${author} in <cite>${cite}</cite>
        </figcaption>
    </figure>`
return markup
})
```

All the Markdown content that is passed into the paired shortcode will be properly rendered as HTML inside the new HTML structure we defined in the plugin. This includes things such as list items, which normal Markdown blockquotes would struggle to properly format.

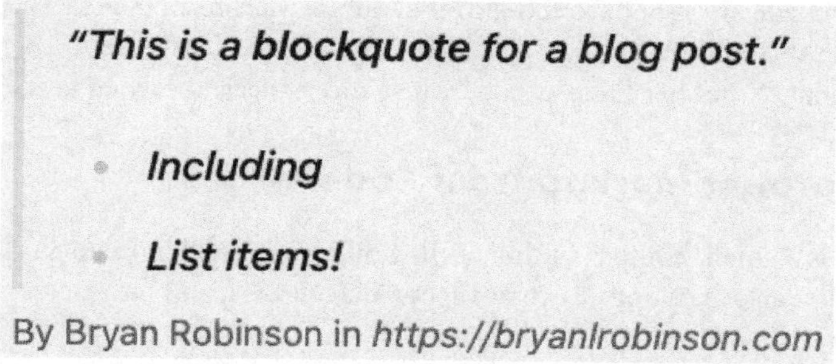

Figure 5.5 – The blockquote being rendered with all the appropriate styles and HTML tags including list items

From here, we can continue adding new features. If you want the ability to have these blockquotes float in your text instead of being a full-width element, we can add a "float" feature to the shortcode. The `float` property will be false by default. That way, when we populate it, we can add a new Tailwind class to the figure to float it left or right depending on the value of the `float` property:

```
eleventyConfig.addPairedShortcode("blockquote",
    (content, author, cite, float=false) => {
    const contentHtml = markdownIt().render(content);
    const markup = `
    <figure class="blockquote ${float ?
        `float-${float}` : ""}">
        <blockquote>
            ${contentHtml}
        </blockquote>
        <figcaption class="blockquote cite">
            By ${author} in <cite>${cite}</cite>
        </figcaption>
    </figure>`
    return markup
})
```

This helps make a blockquote in Markdown significantly more useful for various types of design.

Now that we've extended the default Markdown functionality, let's combine these two examples into one more complex example: a CodePen embed with additional options.

Creating a CodePen embed

The CodePen shortcode takes what we've learned in the past two examples and combines them. In this example, we'll create an embed from the code sandbox website CodePen. There are a lot of great options to tweak in the embed, so having them as arguments in a shortcode helps, and creating a fallback in the content of the shortcode lets us create a nice experience when JavaScript isn't available.

Getting the proper markup from CodePen

On any pen, there is a small "embed" button at the bottom. This will pop up a full editor for how to display the pen with various options, such as theme, default tabs, and more.

Figure 5.6 – The CodePen embed screen showing the style of the pen and all the variables available

For the shortcode, we'll focus on the fallback (the content inside the element that the CodePen script will replace), the theme, default tabs, and height. The script that CodePen uses refers to a username and a slug-hash to determine what pen to embed. That means we'll need both pieces of data to create the embed. Instead of requiring these to be input separately, we can use CodePen's URL structure and get that information from the link to the pen.

With that in mind, let's build the shortcode.

Building the shortcode

Just like before, we'll add a paired shortcode with the addPairedShortcode method and name this one codepen:

```
eleventyConfig.addPairedShortcode("codepen",
  ( content, url, tabs="html,result", theme="default",
    height="300"  ) => {
    // split and name all the parts of the url from codepen
    const [ protocol, , domain, user, pen, hash ] = url.
```

```
split("/");
        const markup = `<div class="codepen"
        data-height="${height}"
        data-theme-id="${theme}"
        data-default-tab="${tabs}"
        data-slug-hash="${hash}"
        data-user="${user}"
        style="box-sizing: border-box; display: flex;
          flex-direction: column; align-items: center;
            justify-content: center; border: 2px solid;
              margin: 1em 0; padding: 1em;">
            <h3>Your JS is turned off. Please turn it on to
              see the codepen. Here's a screenshot from
                <a href="${url}">the Pen</a></h3>
            <a href="${url}"><img style="max-width:
              100%;box-shadow: 1px 1px 5px #999;" src=
                "https://codepen.io/${user}/pen/${hash}
                  /image/large.png" /></a>
            ${content}
        </div>
        <script async src="https://cpwebassets.codepen.io/
          assets/embed/ei.js"></script>
        `;
        return markup
    })
```

This is a bit more complex but follows the same pattern as before:

- We set reasonable defaults for optional elements tabs, theme, and height
- We create the required markup by mixing the CodePen embed code with the data we're getting from the shortcode
- We then return the markup back to the template

The additional feature here is that we also run through more transformations in JavaScript. To start, we need to get the appropriate data off the URL. In this case, we need the username and the slug from the URL. To get that, we use the JavaScript `split` method to split the URL string on slashes. We can then destructure that array into its various pieces (including a blank item to account for the protocol's //). Since the URL for these doesn't change, we can grab the username and slug from this array position and use those pieces in our data attributes for CodePen.

Instead of just returning the content's HTML from markdown like before, we can also extend this with custom markup to allow a user to know what's happening. In this case, we can add a headline to let the user know their JavaScript has been turned off with a link to the pen. Optionally, you can see in the code, that we've added an image as well. That's because CodePen offers a handy URL for getting a screenshot of a pen. In this case, we just need our `url` variable and `/image/large.png` to get a large PNG image of the pen – perfect for encouraging users to click through to see it. After the image, we can add any additional information via the content of the paired shortcode.

Once we have this added to our configuration file, we can add it to any Markdown, Liquid, or HTML file:

```
{% codepen "https://codepen.io/brob/pen/bMqBgb" %}
I'd love to see you there!
{% endcodepen %}
After being added to a page, we can then see the CodePen displayed. If
you turn JavaScript off in your browser, you'll also see a functioning
area with the text we put in the Paired Shortcode.
```

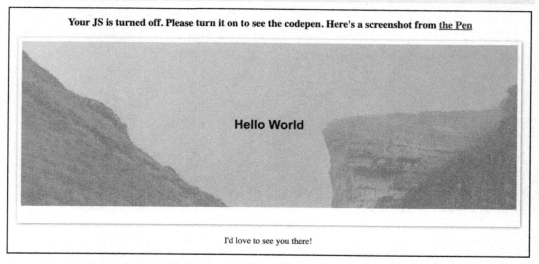

Figure 5.7 – The embedded pen showing the static image from CodePen and a
message informing the user that JavaScript is not enabled to show the full pen

With that, we have three distinct examples of shortcodes for use in a more interactive, media-centric blog.

Summary

In this chapter, we took a look at the various use cases for 11ty's custom shortcodes. Each shortcode is just a wrapper around four of 11ty's template engines' custom tag functionality. We used the `addShortcode` and `addPairedShortcode` methods to create "universal" shortcodes for use in all four of those. In doing so, we used data pulled from attributes as well as content between shortcodes to customize our blog.

In the next chapter, we'll go from a standard blog to an image-based photography site. To do this, we'll dive into the powerful 11ty Image plugin to create multiple views and sizes for each image to always serve the right image at the right time.

Building a Photography Site with the 11ty Image Plugin

Images are one of the biggest concerns for performance on the internet. Even with the large amount of JavaScript most sites ship with, image optimization is the easiest way to increase the speed of your website. Making a photography site with performant images isn't an easy task on your own. Luckily, 11ty has an Image plugin that makes it a bit easier.

In this chapter, we'll review setting up a site that uses collections, dive into a complex use case for JavaScript data files to make image data generation easier, and then explore the Image plugin for setting up proper image formats and sizes for multiple styles of photo blog template, all with a focus on performance.

We'll cover the following:

- Setting up the basic project with collections
- Writing a data file to automatically create an image array for each post
- Installing and configuring the Image plugin
- Creating a specialized template for each Gallery view

Technical requirements

This chapter starts work on a self-contained project. To follow along closely, you can use this book's GitHub repository at `https://github.com/PacktPublishing/Eleventy-by-Example` and open the `start` directory for `project-3`. Additionally, knowledge of both Node.js and client-side JavaScript will help your understanding of the more advanced topics of the chapter.

Setting up the basic project with collections

Let's start by reviewing what we learned in *Chapters 4* and *5* and set up a collection for our photo posts. To get things properly configured, add a new directory in the `src` directory and name it `posts`. This is where we can store all the posts for the photo blog.

Each post can start with three pieces of frontmatter: `title`, `description`, and `date`:

```
---
title: This is the first gallery
description: This is a gallery of kittens
date: "2022-11-01"
---
```

For our photo site, we'll deviate a little bit from the traditional way of creating these new posts and instead of putting the Markdown file directly in the `posts` directory, we'll create a subdirectory with the post slug as its name. In that directory, the post will be added with the name `index.md`. This will allow us to colocate the post's images with the post markdown.

Your posts directory should look like the following structure:

```
- posts
  - post-1-slug
    - index.md
  - post-2-slug
    - index.md
  - post-3-slug
    - index.md
```

To collect everything into one collection, each post will need a `tags` array. We'll accomplish that with a directory data file. Inside the `posts` directory, create a new file named `posts.11tydata.js`. Remember from *Chapter 2* that this will provide any data returned from this file to all the children of this directory. While we don't need this to be an asynchronous JavaScript function, in the next section, we'll do some more JavaScript in this file and need it then.

This JavaScript object sets a default layout and the `tags` array we need for the collection:

```
module.exports = async function() {
    return {
        layout: "layouts/post.html",
        tags: ["posts"]
    }
}
```

The starting code for this project doesn't include a `post.html` layout, so let's create one now. In the `src/_templates/layouts` directory, create a `post.html` file with the following code. This primarily just sets a custom container around the content of the page and, if there's a title set in the frontmatter, displays that with an `h1` element:

```
{% include 'includes/header.html' %}
<div class="container max-w-3xl px-4 mx-auto pt-20 prose">
    {% if title %}<h1>{{ title }}</h1>{% endif %}
```

```
        {{ content }}
    </div>
    {% include 'includes/footer.html' %}
```

Finally, let's make two list areas: a posts page and a section on the home page to pull these new posts in.

In `src/posts.html`, we do a very simple page with a list of post titles with the base layout:

```
---
layout: layouts/base.html
---

<ul>
{% for post in collections.posts %}
    <li>
        <a href="{{post.url}}">{{ post.data.title }}</a>
    </li>
{% endfor %}
</ul>
```

For the home page, we'll add a similar loop but with a visual twist befitting a photo blog. In `src/index.html`, we'll replace the paragraphs under the `<h2>` element containing `Recent Photostories` with the following loop. This code will create a responsive set of cards for each photo post:

```
<ul class="grid gap-3" style="grid-template-columns:
  repeat(auto-fit, minmax(150px, 1fr))">
{% for post in collections.posts %}
    <li class="max-w-sm flex-1 rounded overflow-
      hidden shadow-lg">
        <a href="{{post.url}}" class="block">
            <div class="px-6 py-4">
                <h3 class="font-bold text-xl mb-2">
                    {{post.data.title }}
                </h3></a>
                <p class="text-gray-700 text-base">
                    {{ post.data.description }}
                </p>
            </div>
    </li>
{% endfor %}
</ul>
```

This works and is a nice blog that's ready for content, but there aren't any images yet. We could certainly use Markdown in each of our blog posts to add images to each post, but instead, let's have 11ty create the image data for us in the directory data file.

Writing a data file to automatically create an image array for each post

So, a post with a singular photo isn't a big deal in Markdown. Toss the image URL inside Markdown's image syntax – or better still, use the Image plugin we're installing in the next section – and you're done. If you have an entire gallery of photos for a post, things get bogged down and require a lot of manual work.

For our photo blog, let's create a way to get an array of all the photos available for a specific blog post.

The basic structure of this setup is to have a series of image files in the same directory as the post's Markdown file. Then, we'll use the `posts` directory data file to create an array from all the files. The directory data file is run for each of the documents in the directory, meaning that if we use the `eleventyComputed` functionality, we can compute a unique array for each post.

To start, add a few images to each of your post directories. In the `end` example for this project, we have a series of images from the amazing `placekittens.com`, but any image will work here.

From there, we need to add a script to get all the paths of the images from within these directories to the data for each post. To do this, we'll add a function and an `eleventyComputed` object to the `posts.11tydata.js` file.

The additions start with the inclusion of the Node.js `FileSystem` methods by requiring them at the top of the file. Then, we create a function called `getPaths`. This function accepts the data object that the `eleventyComputed` functionality gives us for each page.

On the data object, each page has a property called `url` that returns the project directory structure starting within the `src` directory. For example, for a post with a slug of `post-1`, `filePathStem` is set to `/posts/post-1/`. While this is the ending URL for the files, our project files live under the `src` directory, so we need to prepend the string `src` to the beginning of this path.

With this constructed path, we can use the `readdir` method on the `fs` object. This will return a list of all files in the directory. Since this could also include further directories, we pass the method an options object with `withFileTypes: true`. This will give additional metadata about each file and allow us to filter based on whether the file is a file or a directory, as well as a regular expression to match the file extension and only include image file extensions. With all the image filenames, we can then rebuild the paths for each one from the page URL and the image name to give us an array of image URLs for use in each blog post:

```
const fs = require("fs")

function getPaths(data) {
    const cwd = "src" + data.page.url
    const files = fs.readdirSync(cwd, { withFileTypes: true })
    const images = files.filter(file => file.isFile() &&
        file.name.match(/\.(jpg|jpeg|png|gif|svg)$/i))
```

```
    const imagePaths = images.map(image => data.page.url +
        image.name)

    return imagePaths
}
```

To add this array to the Data Cascade, we need to add it to the exported function. At the current level of the cascade, we don't have access to all the data we need to run this normally, so we need this to be part of the `eleventyComputed` functionality. This will give us all the data for each post and then add any additional data onto that array. We add an `images` property that passes `data` into a function that returns the value from the `getPaths()` function we just added to the top of this file:

```
const fs = require("fs")

function getPaths(data) {
    const cwd = "src" + data.page.url
    const files = fs.readdirSync(cwd, { withFileTypes: true })
    const images = files.filter(file => file.isFile() &&
        file.name.match(/\.(jpg|jpeg|png|gif|svg)$/i))
    const imagePaths = images.map(image =>
        data.page.url + image.name)

    return imagePaths
}

module.exports = function() {
    return {
        layout: "layouts/post.html",
        tags: ["posts"],
        eleventyComputed: {
            images: data => {
                return getPaths(data)
            }
        }
    }
}
```

With this in our data function, we can now loop through all photos for a specific blog post in the Markdown or the post template. For the moment, let's add a loop to the `post.html` layout to display an image for each post.

Open the basic `/src/_templates/layouts/post.html` layout we created previously. Now, instead of just the title and content, we also want to display all the images. Decide whether you want your Markdown content above or below the gallery and then add a `for` tag to loop through all the images in the new data we just created for each post – the key is `images` as created in `eleventyComputed`:

```
{% include 'includes/header.html' %}

<div class="container max-w-3xl px-4 mx-auto pt-20 prose">

{% if title %}<h1>{{ title }}</h1>{% endif %}

    {{ content }}

    {% for image in images %}
        <img src="{{ image }}">
    {% endfor %}

{% include 'includes/footer.html' %}
```

This adds all the images with a standard HTML `<img>` element and should give us a stacked list of photos on each blog post. Unfortunately, they all appear to be broken images. This is because 11ty is not copying the new images over to our `_site` directory as it would the assets from the first project. To fix this, we need to edit the `eleventy.config.js` configuration file with an additional `addPassthroughCopy` method to tell 11ty which non-generated files to copy.

In *Chapter 1*, we just used the `assets` directory. For this, we need to use a glob string. A glob is a path with asterisks in place of various levels or names. In this case, we need to find any file within nested directories inside the `src` directory and whether they have specific file extensions – any of the image extensions we're going to be using:

```
eleventyConfig.addPassthroughCopy("src/**/*.{jpg,jpeg,png,gif}");
```

After adding this, restart the 11ty `serve` command and images should now be visible on the post pages:

Figure 6.1 – A gallery page with a couple of cute placeholder kitten images

While this already looks like we've accomplished our mission, the smallest photo is 1,500 pixels wide but in an area of the site that's only 736 pixels wide. That's an image that's more than twice as big as it needs to be! Let's install the 11ty Image plugin to take care of dynamically resizing our images for their specific use cases.

Installing and configuring the Image plugin

While 11ty doesn't ship with a built-in way of handling images, there is a first-party plugin for doing just that. The plugin generates multiple sizes for images and provides all the data that's needed to use them with HTML's `picture`, `img`, `srcset`, or as background images. It can also create images in multiple image formats from standards such as JPEG, PNG, and new, more performant formats, such as WebP and AVIF. This means we can optimize the size *and* format to create the best performance for our site.

The plugin is installed via npm:

```
npm install @11ty/eleventy-img
```

Once it's installed in the project, we can set up a custom shortcode to use it.

> **Using the plugin in other files**
>
> The plugin is a JavaScript package. This means that while we are going to utilize it using a shortcode, it could be integrated into the site in other ways from custom configurations to data files. Anywhere JavaScript is available in 11ty is a place you could write code for the Image plugin.

In the `eleventy.config.js` file for our project, we'll require the newly installed plugin and set up an async function to create an image based on the path of the image, alt text, a collection of sizes and widths to be used in HTML's `srcset sizes`

To do this, we pass those values as arguments to our shortcode function:

- `src`: The image path is the `src` attribute and is used by the `Image()` method to generate all the different sizes. To pair with our data, we'll need to prepend the `src` directory path to these strings, since the new files will be generated from the source code and not from the built site.

- `alt`: The Image plugin requires alt text for each image, but at the very least it requires an empty string.

- `sizes`: The `sizes` string corresponds to the HTML sizes attribute. This tells the browser a media query such as `max-width: 500px` and an image size. This lets us specify which size image goes for which size screen.

- `widths`: The `widths` array tells the Image plugin what sizes to generate from our original file and also corresponds to the size values of the HTML `srcset` attribute.

We also specify which formats to use. The more formats are listed, the more opportunities there are for the browser to choose the best format. Ideally, you should have one modern format (such as AVIF or WebP) and a legacy fallback format such as JPEG. This way, images are always served, and in modern browsers, the smallest format is used for best performance. In this case, we'll use AVIF and JPEG.

Finally, we pass that information as metadata and pass `imageAttributes` to the `Image.generateHTML` method. This will return a picture element with multiple source elements inside it. Then, we add the shortcode to use that function with the name `image`.

We start with the basic configuration file:

```
// Copy `assets/` to `_site/assets/`
eleventyConfig.addPassthroughCopy("assets");

// Set the source for 11ty to the /src directory
// Otherwise, this defaults to the project root
// This provides a cleaner project structure
return {
    dir: {
        input: "src",
        output: "_site", // This is the default, but
            it's included here for clarity.
        includes: "_templates"
    }
}
}
```

Then add the code for the shortcode:

```
// Import the Image module
const Image = require("@11ty/eleventy-img");

// An async function to initialize Image and return
    generated HTML
async function imageShortcode(src, alt = "", sizes,
    widths = "300,600") {
  // Generate the image and its metadata based on options
  let metadata = await Image("src" + src, {
    widths: widths.split(","),
    formats: ["avif", "jpeg"],
    outputDir: "./_site/img/",
  });
  // Create attributes to use on HTML generation
  let imageAttributes = {
    alt,
    sizes,
    loading: "lazy",
    decoding: "async",
  };
```

```
  // Generate HTML and return it
  return Image.generateHTML(metadata, imageAttributes);
}

module.exports = function (eleventyConfig) {
  eleventyConfig.addCollection("post", (collection) => {
    return collection.getFilteredByTag("posts").reverse();
  });
  eleventyConfig.addShortcode("image", imageShortcode);

  // Copy `assets/` to `_site/assets/`
  eleventyConfig.addPassthroughCopy("assets");
  eleventyConfig.addPassthroughCopy
    ("src/**/*.{jpg,jpeg,png,gif}");

  // Set the source for 11ty to the /src directory
  // Otherwise, this defaults to the project root
  // This provides a cleaner project structure
  return {
    dir: {
      input: "src",
      output: "_site",
// This is the default, but it's included here for clarity.
      includes: "_templates",
    },
  };
};


}
```

We can now use the new image shortcode in our post.html layout.

```
{% include 'includes/header.html' %}

<div class="container max-w-3xl px-4 mx-auto pt-20 prose">

{% if title %}<h1>{{ title }}</h1>{% endif %}

    {{ content }}

    {% for image in images %}
        {% image image "this is an alt" "(max-width: 500px)
```

```
            300px, (max-width: 1000px) 500px, 100vw"
                 "300, 500, 1000" %}
     {% endfor %}

</div>
{% include 'includes/footer.html' %}
```

For each of our images on the posts, we now have the following HTML rendered using the values we specified in the shortcode. The browser will use the first format and tag that it understands. First, it will use AVIF, and then if that isn't supported it will use the JPEG, and if the source tag isn't supported it will use the img tag:

```
<picture>
    <source type="image/avif" srcset="
    /img/PLNV7xuXd0-300.avif   300w,
    /img/PLNV7xuXd0-500.avif   500w,
    /img/PLNV7xuXd0-1000.avif 1000w
    " sizes="(max-width: 500px) 300px, (max-width: 1000px)
       500px, 100vw" />
    <source type="image/jpeg" srcset="
    /img/PLNV7xuXd0-300.jpeg   300w,
    /img/PLNV7xuXd0-500.jpeg   500w,
    /img/PLNV7xuXd0-1000.jpeg 1000w
    " sizes="(max-width: 500px) 300px, (max-width: 1000px)
       500px, 100vw" />
    <img alt="this is an alt" loading="lazy"
        decoding="async" src="/img/PLNV7xuXd0-300.jpeg"
            width="1000" height="666" />
</picture>
```

That's a lot of code that we no longer need to write to get fully responsive images. Because it's built using a shortcode, it can be adjusted for any use case to get images that are the perfect size. Let's put that to work and create a few alternate templates for our photo posts.

Creating specialized layouts for different gallery

We set up a default layout for each of our posts, but what if we want to change up the design for each? We can do that by creating a new layout and using that layout for individual posts.

Creating a side-scrolling gallery

To start, let's create a scrollable gallery template to show the images at a large size and allow a user to scroll from left to right to see all the images.

This is the first gallery

This is where place kittens thrive.

Figure 6.2 – A gallery with a side-to-side scroll for the images

We can accomplish this with some additional Tailwind classes and resizable images. The Tailwind classes will allow the images to sit side by side and we'll make sure the overflow of the browser for this area is allowed to scroll with a Tailwind class as well.

Create a new layout in the _templates/layouts directory named full.html. This will be the layout we can use on certain posts:

```
{% include 'includes/header.html' %}
<div class="container max-w-3xl px-4 mx-auto pt-20 prose">
    {% if title %}<h1>{{ title }}</h1>{% endif %}
    {{ content }}
</div>

<div class="overflow-x-auto flex gap-5 items-center" >
{% for image in images %}
    <div class="max-w-3xl flex-none  overflow-y-auto">
    {% image image "this is an alt" "(min-width: 30em)
      50vw, 100vw" "300, 500, 1000" %}
    </div>
{% endfor %}
</div>

{% include 'includes/footer.html' %}
```

With this template ready, you can add a layout variable to the frontmatter of any post and provide the value layouts/full.html to set the layout. Even though we set a default layout in the JavaScript data file, we can override that for each individual post thanks to the Data Cascade.

Creating a pop-up gallery

A fairly typical pattern with galleries is to have smaller thumbnail images and a larger pop-up image that triggers on click. This is handled by JavaScript, but the image sizes are equally important:

Figure 6.3 – A full-width gallery

Figure 6.4 – The full-width gallery with a pop-up interface for a clicked image

In this template, we need a little JavaScript and a little extra HTML to allow there to be multiple sizes of images ready to be popped up. The main idea of the code is to set up an anchor tag around each thumbnail image with a class that the JavaScript can identify and set a click event for each of them. Then, the JavaScript finds the sibling element that's the hidden large image and toggles a class to display the image. All of this takes place in the 11ty loop to allow for unique identifiers of each image and each popup.

If writing it in plain JavaScript isn't your thing, any JavaScript library that lets you create pop-up galleries can be used in this same method. The HTML should be added like we've been adding it, and the JavaScript should go right before the footer `include` to allow the markup to be loaded into the DOM before the JavaScript is interpreted.

This layout should be added to the `_templates/layouts` directory and be named `gallery.html`:

```
{% include 'includes/header.html' %}
<div class="container max-w-3xl px-4 mx-auto pt-20
    prose mb-5">
    {% if title %}<h1>{{ title }}</h1>{% endif %}
    {{ content }}
</div>
<div class="grid grid-cols-3 gap-5 flex-wrap gallery">
    {% for image in images %}

    <div class="w-full">
        <a class="opener" data-index="{{forloop.index}}"
            href="{{ image }}">
            {% image image "this is an alt" "(max-width:
                900px) 300px, (max-width: 1500px) 500px,
                100vw" "300, 500, 900" %}
        </a>
        <div tabindex="-1" aria-hidden="true"
            class="modal modal{{forloop.index}} fixed top-0
            left-0 right-0 bottom-0 z-50 bg-gray-700/[.75]
                hidden w-full p-4 overflow-x-hidden
                overflow-y-auto md:inset-0 h-modal md:h-full">
            <button type="button"
                class="closeButton text-gray-100
                    bg-transparent hover:bg-gray-200 hover:
                        text-gray-900 rounded-lg text-4xl p-1.5
                            ml-auto inline-flex items-center
                                dark:hover:bg-gray-600
                                    dark:hover:text-white"
                data-modal-toggle="defaultModal">
                <svg aria-hidden="true" class="w-10 h-10"
                    fill="currentColor" viewBox="0 0 20 20"
```

```
                         xmlns="http://www.w3.org/2000/svg">
                         <path fill-rule="evenodd"
                            d="M4.293 4.293a1 1 0 011.414 0L10
8.586l4.293-4.293a1 1 0 111.414 1.414L11.414 1014.293 4.293a1 1 0 01-
1.414 1.414L10 11.414l-4.293 4.293a1 1 0 01-1.414-1.414L8.586 10 4.293
5.707a1 1 0 010-1.414z"
                            clip-rule="evenodd"></path>
                     </svg>
                     <span class="sr-only">Close modal</span>
                  </button>
                  <div style="top: 50%; transform:
                     translateY(-50%)"
                        class="relative m-auto w-full h-full
                           max-w-6xl md:h-auto">
                     <!-- Modal content -->
                     <div class="relative bg-white rounded-lg
                        shadow dark:bg-gray-700">
                           {% image image "this is an alt"
                              "(min-width: 30em) 50vw, 100vw"
                                 "1000, 1500" %}
                     </div>
                  </div>
               </div>
            </div>

      {% endfor %}
</div>
<script>
      const openers = document.querySelectorAll('.opener');
      openers.forEach(opener => {
            opener.addEventListener('click', function (e) {
                  e.preventDefault();
                  const index = this.dataset.index;
                  const modal = document.querySelector
                     (`.modal${index}`);
                  modal.classList.remove('hidden');
            });
      });
      const closeButtons = document.querySelectorAll
            ('.closeButton');
      closeButtons.forEach(closeButton => {
            closeButton.addEventListener('click', function (e) {
                  e.preventDefault();
                  const modal = this.closest('.modal');
                  modal.classList.add('hidden');
            });
```

```
      });
</script>
{% include 'includes/footer.html' %}
```

With these additional layouts in place, you have a full customizable photo blog set up. You can extend this by adding new layouts, creating new posts, and trying new JavaScript libraries to customize things to your taste.

Summary

In this chapter, we took a look at using the 11ty Image plugin to generate images and HTML for images for a photo blog. We set up a JavaScript data file to generate image data based on images inside of a directory and then passed that information to the Image plugin to generate more image sizes and formats that could be used in both the standard display as well as two additional layouts.

In the next chapter, we'll continue working with 11ty plugins to create a podcast website complete with properly formatted RSS feeds for a podcast and explore what a plugin is.

Building a Podcast Website with 11ty Plugins and Custom Outputs

Not every website is built from just HTML. While HTML is the workhorse of the web, sometimes we need other formats.

In this chapter, we'll dive into the wonderful world of RSS to create a website for a podcast. RSS has been around since 1999 and stands for "Really Simple Syndication." In other words, it's the proper format to provide data to other platforms. In fact, podcasting as we understand it today would never have happened without RSS.

While audio files weren't new to the web, the mixture of audio files with the syndication options allowed with RSS created the first wave of podcasts and podcast directories. When Apple created functionality in iPods to play podcasts, they fully went with RSS for the format of how podcasts would be shared — going as far as to add custom RSS tags that would augment podcast display in their directories.

To build out a full podcast website, we need to embrace both HTML and RSS. Luckily, 11ty is set up to handle that for us. We'll create a custom output for the data we create in an episode collection to live alongside the HTML pages we create. In doing so, we'll need to explore the custom tags that Apple (and other podcast apps) requires for proper formatting. Some of those tags would require significant coding to make them work. Luckily for us, 11ty has a plugin ecosystem and many of the challenges have already been solved. We'll cover the following topics in the chapter:

- Understanding the technical requirements of a podcast website
- What is an 11ty plugin?
- Finding 11ty plugins

- Using the 11ty RSS plugin

- Using the 11ty Podcast Tools plugin

Once you understand the basics of how outputs and plugins work, any new format is within reach – such as JSON, which we'll write in *Chapter 8*. With that, let's dive into the code.

Technical requirements

This chapter starts the fourth project of the book. In order to follow along, you'll need to clone the start directory from the companion repository at `https://github.com/PacktPublishing/Eleventy-by-Example`.

This project start has a few more additions to what has gone into the last two projects. While the blog and photography projects had you set up a collection from scratch for the posts, we won't rehash that need in this chapter. This project comes with an episode directory with the first episode and all the data needed to have the episode pages built by default. Each episode has a `frontmatter` variable named `audioUrl` that contains the path to the file in the project. This variable is used in an HTML audio player that is created as an include in the project.

There's also an additional assets directory named `media` that contains an MP3 used for testing throughout this chapter. This can be replaced with your own content or added to for additional episodes.

In addition to the assets and collection, there's also a global data file in the `src/_data` directory that houses some important information. This will be where you customize your site with your name, email, site name, and more metadata for the podcast.

> **Podcast categories**
>
> It's important to note that the `Categories` array needs to have special categories and shouldn't be any idea you have. Typically, podcasters stick to Apple's list of categories and subcategories. Pick two or three from their list to get started: `https://podcasters.apple.com/support/1691-apple-podcasts-categories`

The following code is an example of the structure of a typical podcast RSS feed:

```
{
    "url": "https://mypodcast.com",
    "name": "My Podcast",
    "authorName": "My Name",
    "authorEmail": "me@myemail.com",
    "description": "This is my amazing podcast",
    "categories": ["Technology", "News", "Tech News"]
}
```

When you're ready to start coding in this chapter, open the directory and run `npm run dev` in your terminal as we've done previously, and there will be a site with a single episode ready to work.

Understanding the special requirements for a podcast site

While a podcast's website may seem on the surface to be just another website, the data requirements to push that content out to multiple platforms are a bit more complex. In order to be on multiple podcast repositories, a podcast needs to have a properly formatted RSS feed with specific data for both the podcast as well as each episode.

This requires additional data and specific formats for the data.

Since we typically build for the web, we usually keep our URLs as relative paths for the project, such as `/episodes/my-first-episode/`. These work perfectly for how the web works. Each browser knows this is relative to the root domain of the website the user is viewing. When pushing your content out to additional places, the paths need to be absolute, such as `https://mypodcast.com/episodes/my-first-episode/`.

Podcast applications also have additional requirements for data and formatting, such as the following:

- Dates formatted in RFC 822
- Proper categorization
- Author information
- Audio file size
- Global updated date
- All wrapped up in XML, not HTM
- While some of this is possible in a regular 11ty site, we need to do some extra configuration and include additional features to make this the most efficient process. To do that, we'll take a trip to the 11ty plugin ecosystem.

What is an 11ty plugin?

The word **plugin** is loaded with context and history. Many systems have implemented a plugin architecture for making changes to the core functionality of a product. Everything from web browsers to desktop applications to content management systems has something they call plugins, each with a variable amount of power over the core software.

The 11ty website defines plugins slightly differently:

> *"Plugins are custom code that Eleventy can import into a project from an external repository."*

This still doesn't quite clear up what an 11ty plugin is.

At its base, an 11ty plugin is a portable configuration that can be added to an 11ty project. What this means is that anything that you can do within the 11ty configuration file, a plugin can do and be added to your project. This includes things such as shortcodes, filters, global data, data transformations, and more.

What this means for our project is that we can pick up the custom functionality needed to make our RSS feed without having to develop it ourselves. Where can we find new plugins?

Finding 11ty plugins

While there's no central repository for 11ty plugins, there are a few ways of finding plugins online.

The first is the official 11ty website. Alongside information on creating and using plugins, `11ty.dev/docs/plugins` contains a list of official and community-contributed plugins. While many are listed here, not all community-created plugins are listed.

In an effort to create a centralized, open source repository, I also created a space for plugins to be found: `plug11ty.com`. Unfortunately, due to the large number of 11ty plugins that have been made, this also isn't a full list.

Luckily, by their nature, 11ty plugins are npm packages. That means by searching `npmjs.com`, you can find any 11ty plugin. By convention, most plugin names begin with the `eleventy-plugin-` string to make searching easier. Both of the plugins we need can be found by searching on the npm site.

For our podcast site, we need two plugins: `eleventy-plugin-rss` and `eleventy-plugin-podcast-tools`.

The RSS plugin provides multiple filters to help with date formatting, absolute URLs, and globally updated time stamps for the whole feed.

The Podcast Tools plugin has a filter to read a local audio file and get its file size for use in the podcast feed.

Using the RSS plugin

To start customizing our project, we need to install and use the RSS plugin. The information we'll need from this plugin is the same as that we'd need to have a traditional RSS feed for a blog as well. To get started, we need to install and configure the plugin.

Installing the plugin

The RSS plugin is an official 11ty plugin and full documentation can be found on the 11ty documentation site. To install the plugin, we need to run an `npm install` command for the npm package:

```
npm install @11ty/eleventy-plugin-rss
```

This will save the plugin to our project and update our `package.json` file. Next, we need to add this to our 11ty configuration file. Just as in the previous projects, the configuration is in the `.eleventy.js` file at the root of the project.

To configure the plugin, we set a new variable at the top of the configuration file and then use the `addPlugin` method inside the exported function of the file:

```javascript
const pluginRss = require("@11ty/eleventy-plugin-rss");

module.exports = function(eleventyConfig) {
    eleventyConfig.addPlugin(pluginRss);

    // Copy `assets/` to `_site/assets/`
    eleventyConfig.addPassthroughCopy("assets");

    // Set the source for 11ty to the /src directory
    // Otherwise, this defaults to the project root
    // This provides a cleaner project structure
    return {
        dir: {
            input: "src",
            output: "_site",
// This is the default, but it's included here for clarity.
            includes: "_templates"
        }
    }
}
```

Now that the plugin is installed, we can start using the filters to begin to solve the needs of our podcast feed.

Setting up a feed page

In our `src` directory, we need to create a new page dedicated to the RSS feed. The RSS plugin is created for use in the Nunjucks template engine. Even though the rest of our site is being rendered by Liquid, this specific template can be rendered with Nunjucks by giving it the proper file extension: `feed.njk`.

Let's start by adding the very basics of an RSS feed to this file. This code starts by defining that this is an XML document and is using XML version 1.0 and RSS version 2.0 – the correct versions for acceptance in iTunes:

```xml
<?xml version="1.0" encoding="UTF-8"?>
<rss version="2.0">
  <title>{{ site.name }}</title>
  <link href="{{ site.url }}{{ permalink }}" rel="self" />
  <link href="{{ site.url }}/" />
</rss>
```

After saving this, a new directory will appear in our `_site` directory and a new route will be available in the localhost. The problem with this is that instead of creating an XML file and route, 11ty has built a file whose content is XML but whose file extension is HTML. This will create issues with most podcast apps, and even Google Chrome displays it as a blank HTML page instead of as data from XML.

This is because 11ty treats everything by default as HTML. We can override this by changing the permalink setting by changing the property in the file's frontmatter. This will change the file placement and extension to an XML document instead of HTML. After saving this file, you can open up `localhost:8080/feed.xml` and Chrome will now recognize this as a feed:

```
---
permalink: '/feed.xml'
---
<?xml version="1.0" encoding="UTF-8"?>
<rss version="2.0">
  <title>{{ site.name }}</title>
  <link href="{{ site.url }}{{ permalink }}" rel="self" />
  <link href="{{ site.url }}/" />
</rss>
```

Once this new page is saved, we can navigate to `http://localhost:8080/feed.xml` and see the output directly:

This XML file does not appear to have any style information associated with it. The document tree is shown below.

```
▼<rss version="2.0">
  <title>My Podcast</title>
  <link href="https://mypodcast.com/feed.xml" rel="self"/>
  <link href="https://mypodcast.com/"/>
</rss>
```

Figure 7.1 – The very simple RSS output displayed in Chrome

Now that we have a properly formatted page, we can start adding all the information needed for the general information for the feed.

To start, we'll add the general information found in the global site data with specific tags for both RSS and iTunes. We'll add tags for the ID, language, author information, description, categories, and image. The main thing to note here is that the description needs to be inside a CDATA field to be valid XML:

```
---
permalink: '/feed.xml'
---
<?xml version="1.0" encoding="UTF-8"?>
<rss version="2.0">
  <title>{{ site.name }}</title>
  <link href="{{ site.url }}{{ permalink }}" rel="self" />
  <link href="{{ site.url }}/" />
  <id>{{ site.url }}</id>
```

```
<language>en-US</language>
<itunes:author>{{ site.authorName }}</itunes:author>
<description><![CDATA[{{ site.description }}]]>
  </description>
<itunes:owner>
  <itunes:name>{{ site.authorName }}</itunes:name>
  <itunes:email>{{ site.authorEmail }}</itunes:email>
</itunes:owner>
<itunes:explicit>no</itunes:explicit>
<itunes:type>episodic</itunes:type>
{% for category in site.categories %}
  <itunes:category text="{{ category }}" />
{% endfor %}

{% if site.image %}
  <itunes:image href="{{ site.image }}" />
  <image>
    <title>{{ site.name }}</title>
    <link>{{ site.url }}</link>
    <url>{{ site.image }}</url>
  </image>
{% endif %}
</rss>
```

The last piece of general information to provide the feed is the updated date. This is where two different filters from the RSS plugin are used.

We need to find the most recently added content item in our episodes collection. We can use the getNewestCollectionItemDate filter for that and then chain that filter with dateToRfc822 to format that date properly. Add the following line to the feed file:

```
<updated>{{ collections.episodes |
  getNewestCollectionItemDate | dateToRfc822 }}</updated>
```

This will display the date in the updated element in the proper format:

```
<updated>Mon, 31 Dec 2018 19:00:00 +0000</updated>
```

Next, we need to loop through all the episodes in the collection and make a discrete RSS item for each. To do this, we need to get the absolute URL for each of the episodes from the relative path provided by 11ty. We do that with Nunjucks' set tag, the post URL, and the RSS plugin's absoluteUrl filter. We also have another instance of an updated date that will require the dateToRfc822 filter again:

```
{% for post in collections.episodes %}
  {%- set absolutePostUrl = post.url | absoluteUrl
    (site.url) %}
```

```
    <item>
      <title>{{ post.data.title }}</title>
      <link href="{{ absolutePostUrl }}" />
      <updated>{{ post.date | dateToRfc822 }}</updated>
      <id>{{ absolutePostUrl }}</id>
    </item>
  {% endfor %}
```

We also need to provide the content from the Markdown file to the feed. This will allow for the transcription and description to be available in various podcast apps. To do this, we can use the `templateContent` variable on each post. If there are any URLs in that content, however, we also need to make those URLs absolute. The RSS plugin has that ready for us with the `htmlToAbsoluteUrls` filter to replace any relative URLs in our Markdown with their absolute versions. Nunjucks also needs to be told to render the Markdown as HTML and not as a string with escaped characters, so we pass that through the `safe` filter:

```
{% for post in collections.episodes %}
  {%- set absolutePostUrl = post.url | absoluteUrl
    (site.url) %}
  <item>
    <title>{{ post.data.title }}</title>
    <link href="{{ absolutePostUrl }}" />
    <updated>{{ post.date | dateToRfc822 }}</updated>
    <id>{{ absolutePostUrl }}</id>
    <content type="html">
      <![CDATA[
    {{ post.templateContent | htmlToAbsoluteUrls
      (absolutePostUrl) | safe }}
  ]]>
    </content>
  </item>
{% endfor %}
```

Finally, each item needs an `enclosure` element. The `enclosure` element provides the actual multimedia content information. This is where we need the Podcast Tools plugin to get the file size information for the feed.

Using the Podcast Tools plugin

Just like the RSS plugin, we need to install this from npm and initialize it in the configuration file:

```
npm install eleventy-plugin-podcast-tools
const pluginRss = require("@11ty/eleventy-plugin-rss");
const podcastTools = require ('eleventy-plugin-podcast-tools');
module.exports = function(eleventyConfig) {
```

```
    eleventyConfig.addPlugin(pluginRss);
    eleventyConfig.addPlugin(podcastTools);
// ... The rest of the configuration file
}
```

Now, we have access to the file size filter. This filter takes a path to a file and if it's an audio file, it will return the size in bytes for valid RSS. Now we have everything we need for a valid `enclosure` tag in our RSS feed. In the loop for each item, add the following code:

```
<enclosure
    url="{{absolutePostUrl}}"
    length="{{ audioPath | filesize }}"
    type="audio/mpeg"
/>
```

With this last item, the project is complete, and you have a fully-functioning podcast website with a properly formatted RSS feed ready to be added to any podcast app.

Summary

In this chapter, we took a basic collections setup within 11ty and added functionality to make a proper RSS feed for inclusion in a podcast directory. This required the installation of two different 11ty plugins. These plugins provided additional functionality like getting a file's size, formatting dates, getting absolute URLs, and more for use in our template. To make the feed, we needed to output an XML file instead of an HTML file. To change this, we used the 11ty permalink functionality to change the filename that 11ty would create.

In the next chapter, we'll extend this project with a custom-built search engine using 11ty Serverless to accept user input and return proper search results on a form submission.

8
Creating a Static-Site Search with 11ty Serverless and Algolia

Accepting user input on a static site is a tricky topic. It's one of the main arguments against the idea of the Jamstack. When all you have is a server that sends HTML and no server-side processing, accepting user input usually ends up relying on client-side code to fill any need for user input. Patterns such as adding comments, like buttons, and search engines are all often dependent on frontend solutions.

While these frontend solutions work, they can often lead to gaps in accessibility, site performance, or search engine optimization. Since they rely on JavaScript, any system that doesn't support JavaScript or doesn't fully support it will not be able to access these solutions. For instance, Algolia has truly amazing and easy-to-use JavaScript libraries to provide powerful search features for a website. However, if a user doesn't have access to JavaScript, they get no search functionality. If we start with a static solution, and then progressively enhance to use the JavaScript version, we can provide a solid experience for all users.

In this chapter, we'll dive into connecting 11ty with a third-party search provider – Algolia – and see how we can leverage 11ty's Serverless plugin to accept user input and generate pages at request time, instead of just at build time. Going static at first will help us overcome the Jamstack's large user input problem. We'll look at the following topics in this chapter:

- Creating a search index from 11ty content
- Setting up 11ty to run in a serverless function
- Creating a search results page
- Querying Algolia at request time on the search page

By the end of the chapter, we'll have a functioning search engine that handles user input, routes that through 11ty's Serverless plugin, and gives search results – all without leaving the 11ty mental model.

Technical requirements

This chapter will continue the work from *Chapter 7* on the podcast website. As such, we'll work from the Project 4 directory in the GitHub companion repository at `https://github.com/PacktPublishing/Eleventy-by-Example`.

Since we're using Algolia as our search index, you'll need to create a free Algolia account to follow along with the chapter. For most small sites, the free account is plenty to get started.

While there are no other requirements for working locally with this chapter, if you wish to deploy this website, a Netlify account and project are recommended. 11ty Serverless can work with other providers, but the defaults are designed to work best with Netlify.

With everything installed and created, we're ready to create our first search index.

Creating a search index from 11ty content

In order for a search to work, a search engine needs a set of data to work from. In this case, we need to create a search index for Algolia to create results based on searches. We can do this in a similar fashion to creating the RSS feed for the podcast in *Chapter 7*. Before we dive into code, let's talk about what Algolia is.

What is Algolia?

Algolia is a software-as-a-service search provider. They provide powerful APIs to create and update a search index, as well as APIs and frontend libraries to build an end user experience. Their search solutions focus on website performance and search accuracy. By default, they have everything we need for a powerful and fast search. In this chapter, we'll only scratch the surface of what Algolia provides with the following features:

- API-driven index creation from JSON
- Serverless access to search results
- Automatic content snippets and highlights for results

Before we dive into Algolia's code, we need to configure 11ty to create a JSON file that we can send to Algolia.

Creating the search JSON file

To start, we'll create a new file to handle the JSON creation. In the _src/ directory, add a new file named `algoliaIndex.njk`. This will generate an HTML file by default, much like the RSS feed in *Chapter 7*. To change this, we need to create a permalink value in our front matter:

```
---
permalink: 'algoliaIndex.json'
---
```

This will ensure that instead of the default HTML, we'll instead get a JSON file.

From there, we need to loop through any content we want to be available in our search and create an object for each piece, with the data Algolia needs to create search results.

To do this, we'll create an array in the file and loop through the episodes collection. Each result needs to have an absolute path for its URL, so we'll use the `absoluteURL` filter we used in *Chapter 7* to generate this.

We can then create an object for each episode. We need to send the data needed to search (title and content), any data to display the results properly (date and URL), as well as a unique identifier named `objectID` for Algolia to keep things distinct. In our case, we can use the default page data to get a slug for our page and use this as the object's ID, since each slug should be unique.

Finally, for this to be valid JSON, we need each episode to have a comma after its end bracket, but the last episode should not have a comma. To accomplish this, we can use the built-in `not` operator and the `loop.last` variable to conditionally add a comma, as long as the episode isn't the last item in the array:

```
---
permalink: 'algoliaIndex.json'
---
[
{% for episode in collections.episodes %}
{%- set absolutePostUrl = episode.url |
    absoluteUrl(site.url) %}
    {
        "objectID": "{{ episode.data.page.fileSlug }}",
        "title": "{{ episode.data.title }}",
        "date": "{{ episode.data.date }}",
        "url": "{{absolutePostUrl}}",
        "content": "{{ episode.content}}"

    }{% if not loop.last %},{% endif  %}
{% endfor %}
]
```

This gets us close, but we've still not created a valid JSON file. When you generate the content from 11ty, you get all the HTML and quotation marks and special characters from the Markdown conversion. This will break our JSON file. To fix this, we can set up a couple of specialized filters to modify the string, making it appropriate for the Algolia search in the following section.

Creating jsonify and htmlStrip filters

To correct these issues, we need to strip all HTML tags, as they're not appropriate for searching in Algolia, and create a JSON-safe string from the content. We can do this with two simple filters, created in the `eleventy.config.js` configuration file.

The `jsonify` filter will take the string of content passed to it and run JavaScript's native `JSON.stringify` method.

The `htmlStrip` filter will use a JavaScript replacement on the content and a regular expression to find all start and end HTML tags, replacing them with a blank string. This will make the content a plain text string.

> **Many thanks to Raymond Camden from the 11ty community**
>
> Raymond Camden is one of the most prolific authors in the 11ty community. In his articles about 11ty and Algolia, he suggests both of these methods. You can find his Algolia article here and see how he handles the process, as there are a few differences in approach – both being valid, depending on your use case: `https://www.raymondcamden.com/2020/06/24/adding-algolia-search-to-eleventy-and-netlify`.

You'll need to add both of these filters to your exported configuration file with the `addFilter()` method we used in previous chapters:

```
eleventyConfig.addFilter("jsonify", function(content) {
    return JSON.stringify(content);
})

eleventyConfig.addFilter("htmlStrip", (content) => {
    return content.replace(/(<([^>]+)>)/gi, "");
})
```

Once these filters are added, we can use them in the `/src/algoliaIndex.njk` template on the content string. We'll start by stripping the HTML and then run it through the `stringify` filter. The order of filters matters; each filter takes the output of the last:

```
---
permalink: 'algoliaIndex.json'
---
[
{% for episode in collections.episodes %}
```

```
{%- set absolutePostUrl = episode.url | absoluteUrl
    (site.url) %}
    {
        "objectID": "{{ episode.data.page.fileSlug }}",
        "title": "{{ episode.data.title }}",
        "date": "{{ episode.data.date }}",
        "url": "{{absolutePostUrl}}",
        "content": "{{ episode.content | htmlStrip |
            jsonify }}"

    }{% if not loop.last %},{% endif  %}
{% endfor %}
]
```

Now, we have a JSON file, and these objects are all formatted to be accepted in an Algolia index. How do we get the data to Algolia? To start, we need to set up our Algolia account.

Setting up Algolia

When you first create your Algolia account, you'll be presented with an "onboarding" flow. We can skip that for now by going to the **Application** dropdown at the top left of the page. There will already be an application created for you. It's named **unnamed application**. Feel free to change that, but it won't affect our progress to have it unnamed:

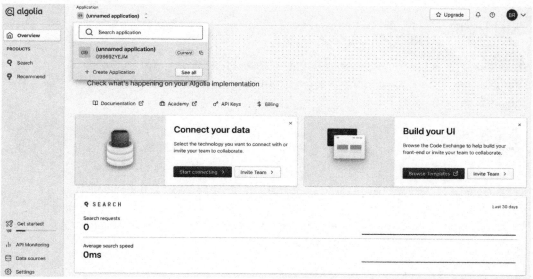

Figure 8.1 – The Algolia dashboard for the Application we just created

When you click on that, you'll be presented with the dashboard for that application, with the metrics for it. On the left, there's a navigation area where you'll click on the **Search** link:

Figure 8.2 – The Search section for our application

This will bring you to the search dashboard for this project. The message will tell you that you don't have any search indices yet and give you a button to create one. Click that button:

No indices yet

An index is an entity within Algolia where you import the data you want to search (indexing) and perform queries against (search).

Figure 8.3 – We don't have indices yet. To make the first one, click the button on this screen

Name your index. I chose the name `episodes` to describe what we're searching for:

Create Index   ✕

> ⓘ To handle indices across multiple environments, just prefix/suffix your index
> name like dev_NAME, test_NAME, or prod_NAME.

Index name

episodes

Create

Figure 8.4 – The Create Index screen

Once you click on **Create**, you'll be taken to the dashboard for that search index. There are no records available. A record is a discrete document for each of our episodes — the JSON objects we created with our 11ty file. We haven't sent those objects yet, so it makes sense that there are no records:

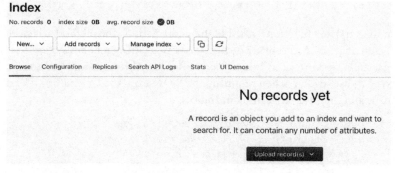

Figure 8.5 – The new search index with no records

At this point, we can add our records in one of a few ways. We could add them manually as JSON in the **Index** dashboard. We could upload the generated JSON from 11ty. Both of these are very manual processes and don't make sense for long-term usage. Instead, let's use the Algolia API to send the records when 11ty is building. This will automate the process so that as we add new episodes, each episode gets added when the site gets built.

Sending records to Algolia

There are a few different ways to handle sending records to Algolia. We could write a bash script to run as part of our build scripts or write a Node script to run at a similar time. While both of these will work and may be preferable to keep things fully portable, we can also use a built-in 11ty feature to add to the actual 11ty build process.

The `eleventyConfig` object has a method named `.on()`. This method allows us to write code that will execute before or after 11ty builds.

> **Eleventy events**
>
> This method is called `Eleventy events`. The events have additional data to make writing this code more streamlined, giving information such as build context (serve, build), and output and input directory information: `https://www.11ty.dev/docs/events/`.

The basic flow of this function is to run after 11ty builds the files to the `_site` directory, get the JSON object from the built files, and then send the contents of that file to Algolia using the `algoliasearch` NPM package:

1. To start, install `algoliasearch`:

    `npm install algoliasearch`

2. Once that's installed, add the package to the top of the `eleventy.config.js` configuration file:

    ```
    const algoliasearch = require('algoliasearch');
    ```

3. Then, in the exported function, we'll add the `.on` method. The method accepts two arguments – an `eleventy.before` or `eleventy.after` string and a function to execute. In our case, we'll use `eleventy.after` and create an asynchronous function to run. We need this to be async to use `await` when requiring the JSON from the `./_site/algoliaIndex.json` path and then pass that into our index:

    ```
    eleventyConfig.on('eleventy.after', async () => {
        const jsonContent = await require
            ('./_site/algoliaIndex.json')
        // ... Algolia code
    });
    ```

    In order to make the client and initialize the index, we need some information from our Algolia application. Since we'll have a write-enabled API key, we'll want to store this information in environment variables.

4. Create a `.env` file in the `root` of the project. This file should be added to the `.gitignore` file, since we don't want to share this data. Then, add the following variables:

    ```
    ALGOLIA_APP_ID="THE-APP-ID"
    ALGOLIA_API_KEY="THE-API-KEY"
    INDEX_NAME="THE-INDEX-NAME"
    ```

    These variables can all be found in your Algolia application. If you've been following along, the index name will be episodes. The other two pieces of data are best found in the **Team and Access** area of your application's settings.

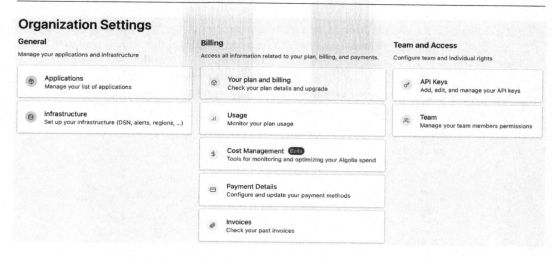

Figure 8.6 – The Organization Settings screen in Algolia

5.   Click **API Keys** to get the information. The **Application ID** information is the first thing on this screen:

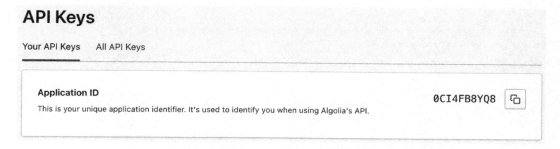

Figure 8.7 – The API Keys screen for our application

After the ID, there are multiple keys. The Admin API key will work but would give full access to our application as an admin. This is, perhaps, less secure than would be prudent. Instead of that key, let's create a special key with the exact permissions we need.

6.   Click **All API Keys** to access the full **API Keys** screen:

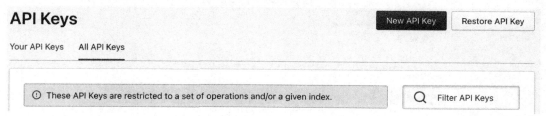

Figure 8.8 – The All API Keys screen

7. Click the **New API Key** button. In the resulting popup, we can provide the exact information required with granular permissions. You can even restrict the validity time period, rate limits, and HTTP referrers for the key. In our case, let's keep all those unlimited. The main thing we'll change is the ACL. This is the list of permissions for the key. By default, this will be just `search`; we also need `browse`, `addObject`, and `listIndixes`. Once you have added these permissions, click the **Create** button:

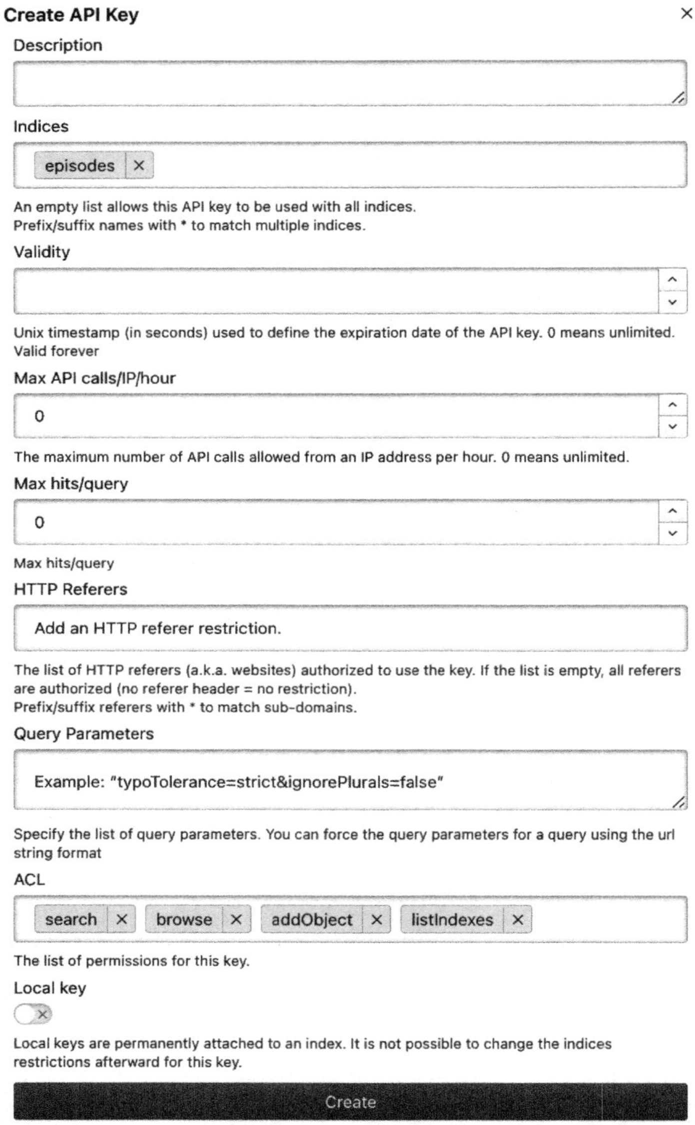

Create API Key   ✕

Description

Indices

episodes ✕

An empty list allows this API key to be used with all indices.
Prefix/suffix names with * to match multiple indices.

Validity

Unix timestamp (in seconds) used to define the expiration date of the API key. 0 means unlimited.
Valid forever

Max API calls/IP/hour

0

The maximum number of API calls allowed from an IP address per hour. 0 means unlimited.

Max hits/query

0

Max hits/query

HTTP Referers

Add an HTTP referer restriction.

The list of HTTP referers (a.k.a. websites) authorized to use the key. If the list is empty, all referers
are authorized (no referer header = no restriction).
Prefix/suffix referers with * to match sub-domains.

Query Parameters

Example: "typoTolerance=strict&ignorePlurals=false"

Specify the list of query parameters. You can force the query parameters for a query using the url
string format

ACL

search ✕   browse ✕   addObject ✕   listIndexes ✕

The list of permissions for this key.

Local key

⊂✕

Local keys are permanently attached to an index. It is not possible to change the indices
restrictions afterward for this key.

Create

Figure 8.9 – The screen to create an API key

8.   Once saved, you can copy the new key for use in the `.env` file.

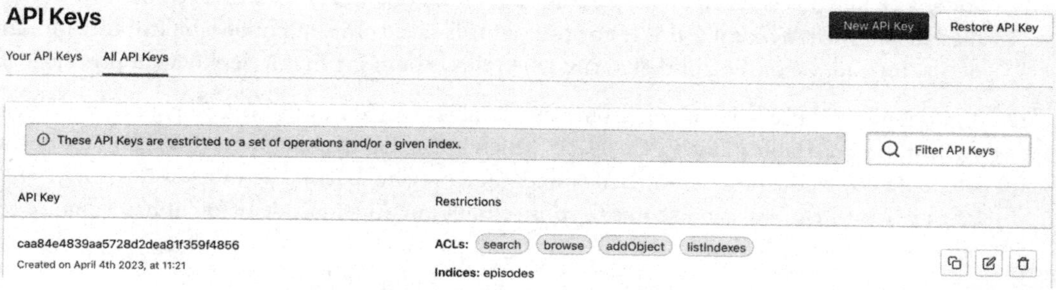

API Keys

Your API Keys   **All API Keys**

[New API Key]   [Restore API Key]

> ⓘ These API Keys are restricted to a set of operations and/or a given index.   [🔍 Filter API Keys]

API Key	Restrictions	
caa84e4839aa5728d2dea81f359f4856 Created on April 4th 2023, at 11:21	**ACLs:** (search) (browse) (addObject) (listIndexes) **Indices:** episodes	🗐 ✏ 🗑

Figure 8.10 – The new API key added to the All API Keys screen

9.   Now that we have the variables, we need a way to access them in our files. To do this locally, we can use the `dotenv` NPM package:

```
npm install dotenv
```

10. Once installed, we need to add this to our configuration file by using a `require` statement at the top of our `eleventy.config.js` file. By running it this way without naming it as a variable, it will automatically configure and give access to environment variables under the `process.env` object:

```
require('dotenv').config();
```

The method takes an app ID and API key to authenticate that we can write to the index. After the client is created, we can then initialize the index in our code by providing the `client.initIndex()` method with our index name.

11. Once we have the data and keys, we need to create a search client by using the `algoliasearch` method created. The client then initializes an index, and then we can save all the objects in our file to the index:

```
eleventyConfig.on('eleventy.after', async () => {
    const jsonContent = await require('./_site/algoliaIndex.
json')

    const client = algoliasearch
        (process.env.ALGOLIA_APP_ID,
            process.env.ALGOLIA_API_KEY);
    const index = client.initIndex
        (process.env.INDEX_NAME);

    index.saveObjects(jsonContent)
});
```

When this runs, it will send the data to Algolia. The next time 11ty runs, it will push data into Algolia. While this is exactly what we want right now, this will also run every time 11ty builds files. When working locally, this is any time a file is saved. This might be a bit extreme for our needs. Instead, we only want this to run when this is building in our deployment process.

12. To do that, we'll use a default environment variable created by our host. In Netlify, we get an environment variable named CONTEXT, which is the deployment context. When building a site to deploy to the production URL – and not a preview URL – the value of CONTEXT will be production. We can use this to short-circuit our Algolia code before it has a chance to build and send to Algolia:

```
eleventyConfig.on('eleventy.after', async () => {

    // Short circuit if we're not in production according
to Netlify
    if (process.env.CONTEXT !== 'production') return

    const jsonContent = await require
        ('./_site/algoliaIndex.json')

    const client = algoliasearch
        (process.env.ALGOLIA_APP_ID, process.env.
            ALGOLIA_API_KEY);
    const index = client.initIndex
        (process.env.INDEX_NAME);

    index.saveObjects(jsonContent)
});
```

Now, the code will only run when building on Netlify's servers and when the context is set to production. This will mainly occur when new content is added or when data has changed.

In this section, we built a search engine with Algolia. To do that, we needed to structure our content into a JSON file that could be imported into Algolia. Once we had that, we needed a way to send that to Algolia. We used 11ty's events to send the JSON file we built to Algolia after a production build. In the next section, we'll use this new search engine to build out search results when a user submits a search form on our site.

Setting up 11ty to run in a serverless function

Typically, on a static site such as the type 11ty creates, there's no way to handle any user input. That sort of thing is reserved for when you have server-side code that you can run. We're using a static site generator on a dedicated static site host. We don't have access to typical server-side architecture.

Instead, we have serverless functions that we can use. While serverless functions are great for handling data and user input, responding with a full HTML page can be cumbersome. Sending back HTML that is the same as what our static HTML was at build time required a lot of rewriting of HTML into JavaScript template literal strings, or the implementation of bigger template libraries in our functions. This was a problem for maintenance. To deal with this, as of the 1.0 release of 11ty, we now have access to a built-in plugin named 11ty Serverless. This allows 11ty to provide all the templates from our build to serverless functions to build pages on demand, with data provided by users.

While this is a plugin, it's one that ships when you install 11ty, so there's no need to run any additional installations.

Configuring 11ty Serverless

Since it's already installed, we just need to add it to our configuration file. At the top of `eleventy.config.js`, add the following line:

```
const { EleventyServerlessBundlerPlugin } = require
    ("@11ty/eleventy");
```

Then, like any other plugin, we'll add it inside the exported function of our configuration. The plugin can be initialized as many times as we want, so this initialization will be specific to our search use case, but you can have multiple serverless pages by initializing with different names.

> **More Serverless features**
>
> In this chapter, we're covering the basics of using the Serverless plugin, but there are plenty of advanced use cases that require a bit more configuration. For all configuration options, see the official documentation for Serverless: `https://www.11ty.dev/docs/plugins/serverless/`.

The main configuration for each initialization of 11ty Serverless is to give an instance a name and a `functions` directory. The name will be used when we build our serverless routes, and the functions directory will be used to tell the bundler where to store all the files necessary to create the serverless functions for us. In this instance, we'll name it `search`, and since we're deploying this to Netlify, we'll follow the Netlify serverless `functions` path and put these files in the `/netlify/functions/` directory in our project. The plugin will create this directory for us, so there's no need to add it manually:

```
eleventyConfig.addPlugin(EleventyServerlessBundlerPlugin, {
name: "search", // The serverless function name for the
    permalink object
functionsDir: "./netlify/functions/",
});
```

The next time 11ty runs, it will create a new folder for the search functions. In our case, this will live in the root of the project at `netlify/functions/search`. If you open that directory, there are a lot of new files. Most of these do not need to be in our GitHub repository. They're intended to be generated by the build process. The only file we need to keep for the repository is the `index.js` file. This file can even be modified and customized in small ways for various serverless methods.

To keep the new files out of the GitHub repository, we need to create (or modify) our `.gitignore` file in the root of the project. To remove the new files, we'll specify that all files in the new directory should be ignored and then make an exception for the `index.js` file:

```
.env
netlify/functions/search/**
!netlify/functions/search/index.js
```

11ty Serverless is now ready to be used. To use it, we need to create a new page. Since we're using it for searching, let's create a dynamic search results page.

Creating the search results page

To start, let's add a new file in the src directory named `search.html`. This will contain all the information we'd normally see on a page, such as a title and layout, as well as any HTML we want to display. In this case, we'll add a search field with some Tailwind classes and an action of `/search/` to send the query to this URL.

The one difference we have is the need for a new permalink. In the previous examples, the permalink had been a single string variable in the front matter of a page. When we use the Serverless plugin, we can create permalinks for various instances. This means we need the permalink to be an object instead of a string. Each key in the object should match the name of a Serverless plugin instance. If desired, you can also use a key of `build` to have the page built statically as well:

```
<form action="/search/" class="input-group relative flex
    items-stretch w-full mb-4">
    <label for="q" class="sr-only">Search</label>
    <input type="search" name="q"  class="form-control relative flex-
auto min-w-0 block w-full px-3 py-1.5 text-base font-normal text-
gray-700 bg-white bg-clip-padding border border-solid border-gray-300
rounded transition ease-in-out m-0 focus:text-gray-700 focus:bg-white
focus:border-blue-600 focus:outline-none" placeholder="Search" aria-
label="Search" aria-describedby="button-addon2">
    <button type="submit" class="btn inline-block px-6 py-2.5 bg-
blue-600 text-white font-medium text-xs leading-tight uppercase
rounded shadow-md hover:bg-blue-700 hover:shadow-lg focus:bg-
blue-700  focus:shadow-lg focus:outline-none focus:ring-0 active:bg-
blue-800  active:shadow-lg transition duration-150 ease-in-out flex
items-center" type="button" id="button-addon2">
```

```
        Search
    </button>

</form>
```

Once saved, you'll have a new page at `/search/` on your site, but there won't be a `search` directory or file in your `_site` directory. It's always built at request time.

Figure 8.11 – The search page on the site.

The search field on this page doesn't do anything but reload the page currently. That's because we're not displaying anything based on user input. Go ahead and search for `episode` in the search field. When it runs, notice that the URL now has query parameters – `http://localhost:8080/search/?q=episode`. The `q` parameter is the name of the form field in our form. Let's add some code to display the query on the page.

Below the form, we'll add `h2` to provide the user with confirmation that they're searching for what they wanted. With the Serverless plugin, we now have access to a new set of data for our templates – `eleventy.serverless`.

On that object, we have a query object and a path object. The query has any query parameter in the URL, and the path object has any piece of the URL path after the route. For our search example, we'll use query parameters, although the path functionality opens up great possibilities as well.

Our `h2` will use this new object to get the value of the `q` parameter from the query parameters and display it on the page. While we're at it, let's set the value of the search input to the query as well. Since we'll use this again in the future, let's set it to an easier variable to use by using Nunjucks' `assign` tag.

Place the `assign` tag just after the frontmatter for the template:

```
{% assign query = eleventy.serverless.query.q %}
```

Then, add the `value` attribute to the search input in the `form` element:

```
<input type="search" name="q" value="{{ query }}"
    class="classes..." placeholder="Search"
    aria-label="Search" aria-describedby="button-addon2">
```

Finally, add an h2 element after the form to show the user their input:

```
<h2 class="is-size-3 mb-3">Searching for "{{ query }}"</h2>
```

We should now see **Searching for "episode"** right beneath the search field. This will change on every search query to match the query entered. Try searching for a different word and see the page change in response to your input.

Figure 8.12 – The search page with a query of episode. This is input and sent to our Serverless template, and then it is able to display as the query from the request

Now, we need to use this query to send a search request to Algolia. In a typical serverless function, we'd just add this to the function as an API call. Since this is 11ty, we have a cleaner way of doing this – a template filter.

Querying Algolia at request time on the search page

The basic flow of this process is to take the query and run it through a new search filter, which will return a list of data from Algolia that we can then loop over in our template:

```
{% assign query = eleventy.serverless.query.q %}
{% assign results = query | search %}
```

The query is passed to the filter and then sent off to Algolia, and the results variable is set to an array of data that comes back. To use this new filter, we need to define it in the configuration function.

Before we start with the code, we need to configure Algolia to tell it what to make searchable. Back in the **Index** dashboard in Algolia, click on the **Configuration** tab.

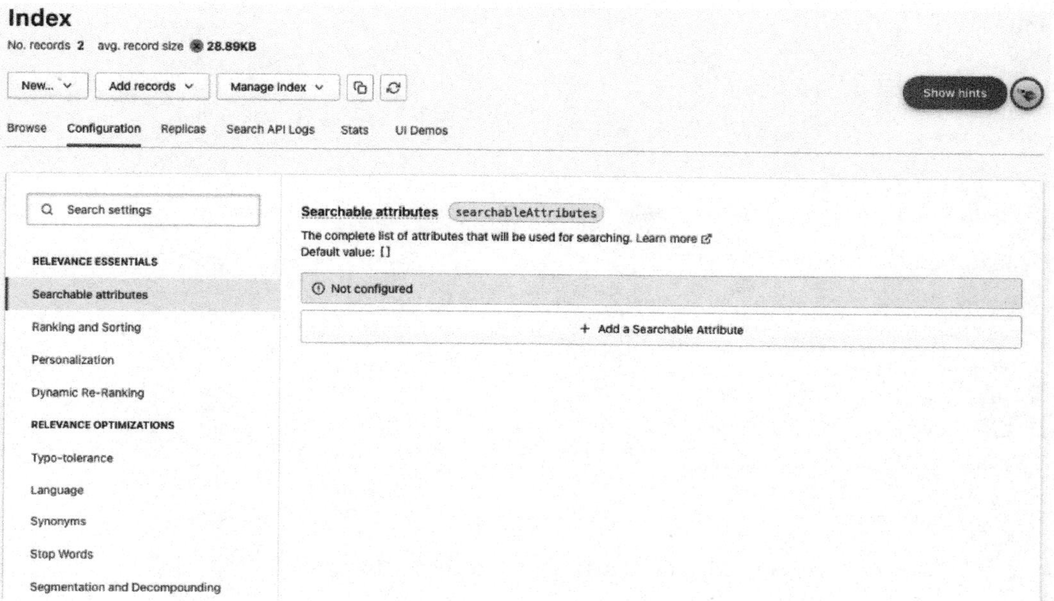

Figure 8.13 – Setting the searchable attributes in Algolia for our search query

From there, we can go to **Searchable attributes** and add the **title** and **content** fields. The order of these attributes will also correspond to the priority in the results. Results with the query in the title should probably rank higher than just the content, but this is where you can tweak the algorithm for your personal search engine.

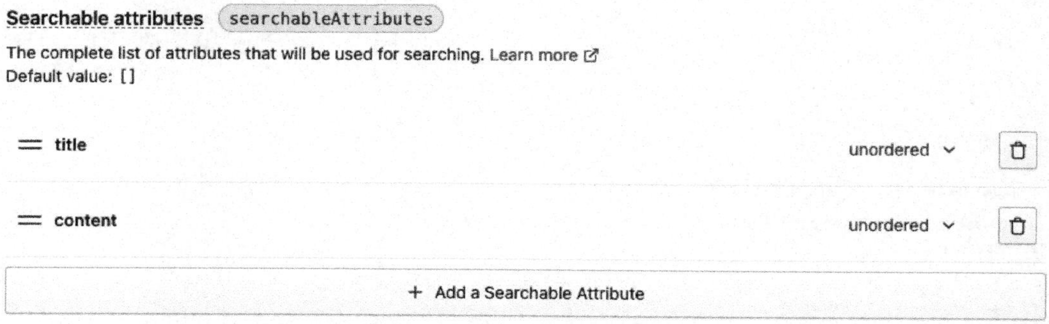

Figure 8.14 – The final view of the searchable attributes

At this point, also add **title** to the highlighting options. This will ensure that results come back with query words wrapped in <em> tags. You can also customize the tags that are used for highlighting. We don't want to use highlighting on the content because it's large. Instead, we'll use Algolia's snippeting feature to get less back in our response.

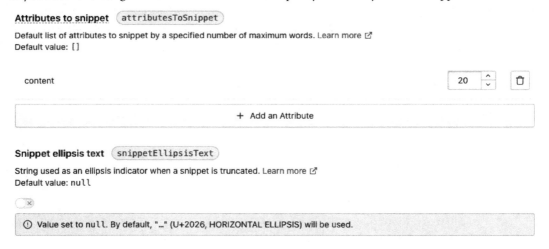

Figure 8.15 – The Algolia settings for highlighting attributes

Add the **content** attribute to the **snippeting** settings. This will allow us to use a snippet from around a keyword inside the entire content of a page to show as a description in our search results — much as you'd see in a Google search result. You can also specify how many words a snippet should have.

Attributes to snippet   (attributesToSnippet)

Default list of attributes to snippet by a specified number of maximum words. Learn more ☑
Default value: []

content   20 ⌃⌄   🗑

+ Add an Attribute

Snippet ellipsis text   (snippetEllipsisText)

String used as an ellipsis indicator when a snippet is truncated. Learn more ☑
Default value: null

(✕

ⓘ Value set to null. By default, "…" (U+2026, HORIZONTAL ELLIPSIS) will be used.

Figure 8.16 – The settings for Attributes to snippet

Once you've made these changes, apply them by clicking the **Review and save** button. When these are set up, we're ready to programmatically query the index.

While we've already added the `algoliasearch` method to this file, it's the full package from Algolia. While this would work, Algolia is all about speed. Since this is happening at request time, we need to also be thinking about speed. Thankfully, Algolia packages a "lite" version in the search package. This lite version is only used to perform searches and has none of the code necessary to perform writes or modifications, but it comes at a much smaller size — important when every byte counts.

At the top of `eleventy.config.js`, we'll create a new variable for the lite version by requiring it from the `/lite/` directory in the NPM package:

```
const algoliasearch = require('algoliasearch');
const algoliasearchlite = require('algoliasearch/lite')
```

Then, we can use it in much the same way we did when writing to the index earlier in the chapter. We initialize the method with our app ID and API key and initialize the index. Then, instead of saving objects, we can use the search method. We can pass that method the query, which is the string the filter is placed on, and then pass it a series of options. The only option we need in our code is to specify the explicit attributes to retrieve. This keeps the response from Algolia as tight as possible, since this is request-time loading.

Since we're not using an async filter, we can use the `.then()` method on the search to return hits – Algolia's name for search results – to send the results to the template:

```
eleventyConfig.addFilter("search", (query) => {
    const client = algoliasearchlite
        (process.env.ALGOLIA_APP_ID, process.env.ALGOLIA_
            API_KEY);
    const index = client.initIndex(process.env.INDEX_NAME);
    return index.search(query, {
        attributesToRetrieve: ["title", "url"],

    }).then(res => {
    return res.hits;
    })
})
```

Each hit has the information we requested, as well as `_snippetResult` and `_highlightResult` objects. These contain the snippeted content and highlighted title respectively, both of which we want to use in the `/src/search.html` template. The following is the structure for the data that Algolia returns:

```
{

    "title": "My first episode",
    "url": "https://mypodcast.com/episodes/
        my-first-episode/",
    "objectID": "my-first-episode",
```

```
    "_snippetResult": {
      "content": {
        "value": "&quot;A little description of the
          <em>episode</em>\nThis is a description\n\n
              \n              \n                    Download
                  audio\n            \n   \n\n\nOur Guest:
                      Salma Alam-Naylor\nWhat she …",
        "matchLevel": "full"
      }
    },
    "_highlightResult": {
      "title": {
        "value": "My first <em>episode</em>",
        "matchLevel": "full",
        "fullyHighlighted": false,
        "matchedWords": [
          "episode"
        ]
      }
    }
  }
}
```

Now that this is available in our template, we can add a results loop. At the same time, we can add a conditional and check whether there is no query or whether the results come back with a length of 0; we can display **No results found**, and if those conditions aren't matched, we can display our h2 and our loop for the results.

Instead of just getting the title and content from the result itself, we can dig deeper into the snippets and highlights and get the value of each to display the custom HTML, making the highlighted words display in italics:

```
{% assign query =  eleventy.serverless.query.q %}
{% assign results =  query | search %}

{% if eleventy.serverless.query.q == undefined or
    results.size == 0   %}
    <p class="is-size-5">No results found</p>
    {% else %}
    <h2 class="is-size-3 mb-3">Searching for "
        {{ eleventy.serverless.query.q }}"</h2>

    {% for result in results %}
        <h3 class="is-size-4 mb-2">
```

```
        <a href="{{ result.url }}">
            {{ result._highlightResult.title.value }}</a>
        </h3>
        <p>{{ result._snippetResult.content.value }}</p>
    {% endfor %}
{% endif %}
```

This gives us back all of our results with the query highlighted.

Figure 8.17 – Search results for episode after building out the result template

We now have a full-fledged, serverless search engine – all without writing a serverless function ourselves and using only 11ty functionality.

Summary

In this chapter, we tackled adding request-time data to a static website without the need for any frontend JavaScript. By using 11ty Serverless, we were able to use all of our hard-earned 11ty knowledge to build out HTML pages on the fly at request time. There was no need for annoying JavaScript templating or a deep understanding of the Node.js runtime.

We used the 11ty RSS plugin with a special permalink and two new custom 11ty filters to create a JSON file appropriate for sending to the search solution Algolia. We sent that off to Algolia via its API and used 11ty's events functionality to resend it every time 11ty builds the site.

We then added a serverless route to our static site so that users could submit a search form and get dynamic content back. This route was built with 11ty's standard templating and the bundled 11ty Serverless plugin. We then took the user input from the search field and sent a query to Algolia to get back properly formatted and weighted search results – all with no client-side JavaScript. If you want to take the user experience further, you can also look into Algolia's frontend JavaScript package InstantSearch to provide a seamless, polished search experience when JavaScript is enabled, but fall back on the solid knowledge learned in this chapter for clients with no JavaScript.

Now that we have a search engine for our podcast, we need to look into making the editing experience even better. In the next chapter, we'll continue our work on this project and add a headless content management system.

9

Integrating 11ty with a Headless CMS

One of the great things about 11ty is that it can be an all-in-one solution for people looking to publish content, do a little development work, and generate HTML; but what if you don't want to store your content in Markdown in your repository? Enter the world of headless **content management systems (CMSs)**.

In this chapter, we'll take our podcast website and add the headless CMS Hygraph as a data source. By decoupling our content from our code, we get a couple of superpowers from Hygraph that allow us to simplify our code, while at the same time simplifying our content editing and writing process. In doing this, we'll explore what a headless CMS is, how to create proper data via content modeling, and how to get that data into our 11ty site. Finally, we'll automate the process of publishing the site by setting it to trigger when a new CMS entry is added or updated to keep our publishing flow simple and clean.

In this chapter, we'll cover the following:

- Why use a headless CMS with 11ty?

- Creating proper data in your CMS

- Querying and formatting the data

- Converting existing pages to use CMS data

- Creating a pagination template to create individual 11ty pages

- Creating a flow to allow new content to republish the site

Technical requirements

This chapter will continue the work from *Chapters 7* and *8* on the podcast website. As such, we'll work from the `Project 4` directory in the GitHub companion repository at `https://github.com/PacktPublishing/Eleventy-by-Example`.

We'll be using Hygraph as our headless CMS, so you'll need to create a free Hygraph account to follow along with the chapter. For most small sites, the free account is plenty to get started.

In using Hygraph, we'll be querying our content data using GraphQL, so a passing familiarity with the query language will be helpful, but not necessary.

Once you have an account with Hygraph and have the repository downloaded, we're ready to dive into the wonderful world of headless content management.

Why use a headless CMS with 11ty?

Markdown is great. I use Markdown in many projects, but it has its limits. When you start moving away from simple text-based content, the syntax becomes more problematic. Often, I find myself injecting HTML into my Markdown — which 11ty allows, by the way — and that ends up defeating the simplicity of Markdown. Add into the mix non-developers and even the simplicity of Markdown syntax is something that becomes a hurdle.

Beyond Markdown, frontmatter is a fine way of managing a small amount of data, but any level of complexity becomes a bit of a headache. A headless CMS can help us overcome both of these limitations.

What is a headless CMS?

You may be familiar with the concept of a content management system. It's a place that stores data and content in an easily editable format. A traditional CMS typically has everything built in: an editing interface, a server-side language, and a way of building templates. This monolithic approach won't necessarily work with the new decoupled way of developing sites.

A headless CMS takes the dashboard from a CMS and, instead of outputting a full website, provides an API for use with any system that can query that API. This is a perfect fit for 11ty. Most headless CMSs come with an idea of content modeling to build how the API will be structured, an API to query, and additional utilities to help manage and transform the data in various ways.

The basic workflow for a headless CMS starts with the creation of a project and content model. The content model will inform how the content is edited, but also how the API is generated. From there, 11ty will ingest the data and that data can be used in any template. This flow will be the same with any headless CMS on the market. The only difference will be how the data is structured in the API, how the API is generated, and the additional tools available.

In this chapter, we'll be using the headless CMS Hygraph to power the episodes on our podcast site.

What is Hygraph?

Hygraph bills itself as a **federated content platform**. This means that it pairs traditional headless CMS features with additional features to help manage multiple APIs in one concise API. It was also the first GraphQL-native CMS on the market. This gives us all the power of a GraphQL API built directly into our CMS, along with strong documentation via an in-CMS API playground to inspect and try various GraphQL queries to figure out the best use for each project.

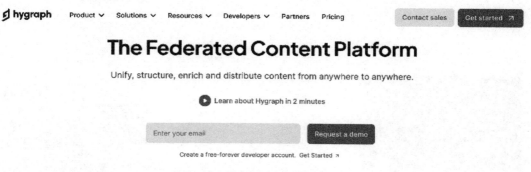

Figure 9.1: The Hygraph home page

The editing interface is streamlined and allows content modeling directly in the project with many built-in field types to make the best content API you can.

Let's dive in and make our project in Hygraph.

Creating proper data in Hygraph

Once you've created an account with Hygraph, it's time to create a project. Each project will correspond to a single set of content models, API endpoints, and users. The original dashboard page has multiple starters we can choose from, but for our purposes, we'll start with a blank project by clicking the **Add Project** button. When creating a project, you'll need to give it a name and an optional description. From there, you can choose where your content is hosted. All content will eventually be served from a global CDN, but the data center should be closest to you to start with.

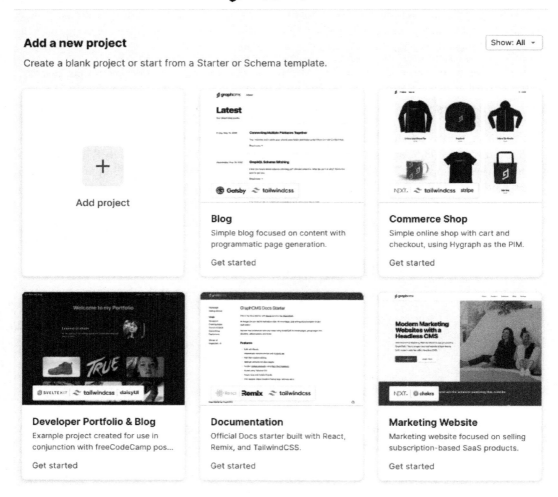

Figure 9.2: The add project interface that's shown after creating an account with Hygraph

Once the project is created, you'll land on the dashboard for the project. From this dashboard, you can navigate on the left of the interface to multiple areas of the application. On the right, there's an onboarding flow that we'll follow for most of this creation process: we'll set up our content model in the **Schema** area, create content in the **Content** area, use the API playground to explore the content API, and then make our API accessible to queries from our 11ty project.

Content modeling in the Schema area

All the data we need to be in the API will be created from the structure that we set in the **Schema** area. Navigate to the **Schema** page, and create a new model from the options presented. We also have the option to create components (reusable models), remote sources (additional API sources), and enumerations (structured lists of content). We won't need any of these in this project.

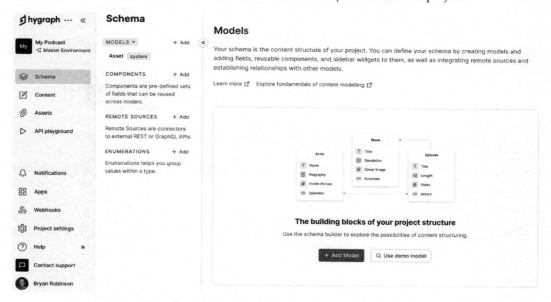

Figure 9.3: The Schema page in Hygraph where we can add our content model

When you add a model, you're asked to give it a display name, API ID (which will generate a plural version), and an optional description. Name your model `Episode`. This will generate a proper API ID and plural ID for you. Then click **Add Model**.

Add Model

Display name
Name that will be displayed in Hygraph

```
|
```

API ID
ID used for accessing this model through the API

Plural API ID
Pluralized API ID for this model

Description (optional)
Displays a hint for content editors and API users

Cancel   Add Model

Figure 9.4: When we add a content model, we get a popup to add some basic details

After we enter these details, we'll be taken to a blank model page. This is where we'll create our collection of fields.

Figure 9.5: A blank model page in Hygraph

All the data we need for each episode needs to be created on this page using the fields that are available on the right. Let's review the data each episode has and map it to a specific field type:

- **Title**: The title should be a single line of text. This can also be marked as the **Title** field to allow it to display in the listing:

  - **Display name**: `Title`

  - **API ID**: `title`

- **Date**: We need a date for this episode to be published. We can use the **Date** field:

  - **Display name**: `Publish Date`

  - **API ID**: `publishDate`

- **Audio File**: Instead of using just a URL for the audio file, we can store the file itself in Hygraph to gain additional data. For this, we can use the `Asset picker` field:

  - **Display name**: `Audio File`

  - **API ID**: `audioFile`

- **Body**: For the main content of each episode, we can choose between two choices: **Rich Text** or **Markdown**. For this demo, we'll use **Rich Text** to get additional options in our API:

  - **Display name**: `Body`

  - **API ID**: `body`

  - **Embeds**: If you wish to have images in your body, enabling embedding allows an editor to choose an image to add. For the demo, I've left this off, but you may choose to allow it for your own content.

- **Slug**: We need to generate a path for 11ty. We won't have the advantage of a filename to generate the URL anymore. The **Slug** field will help us generate a URL based on other fields:

  - **Display name**: `Slug`

  - **API ID**: `slug`

  - **Generate slug from template**: Check this box and, in **Slug template**, include `{title}` to have the slug generate automatically from the **Title** field

The order in which these fields are listed is the order in which they'll display in your content entry, so choose the right order for your editing experience by dragging each field into the right order. Once you've added all the fields, your interface should look like this:

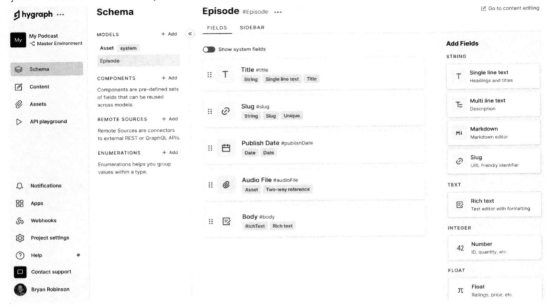

Figure 9.6 – Final state for an Episode in Hygraph

Next, we need to add content to Hygraph.

Adding content to Hygraph

Once the model is in place, click the **Content** navigation item and then click **Add Entry** at the top right of the page. This will take you to a blank content form page with the fields we just generated.

Figure 9.7: The editing interface generated by the content model

Most of these fields are self-explanatory. Since we already have this content, most of it can be copied from the Markdown files for our episodes. The **Body** field, however, needs a little help. Since it's not a Markdown field, any Markdown we paste in will not have the proper styles applied. Instead of copying from our source files, go to the running local site and copy the content from the page in the browser. This will automatically pull in the proper levels of headings and other styles, such as anchor tags, and make your life much easier.

After adding an episode or two into the interface, it's time to run our first query to get a feel for how they work.

Querying the API in the API playground

The **API Playground** link in the navigation pane will take us to a place to test GraphQL queries in the CMS. This is handy for creating queries to then use in our code. The interface has an area to inspect our queries as we build them and include exactly the data we want in the format we want it in.

> **What is GraphQL?**
>
> GraphQL is a query language for APIs that helps developers create requests for just the data they want in the exact shape they need. This is different from normal REST APIs where you make a query and get all the data back.
>
> Find out more at `graphql.org`.

For each episode, we need to get the `publishDate`, `slug`, and `title` fields. We also need to get the body content and audio file information.

The `body` field doesn't just generate a string, it creates an object. That object has multiple versions of our content. There is a raw JSON representation, great for custom displays, a static HTML representation, a Markdown representation, and a pure text representation. For our use cases, we'll take the HTML and the text: HTML for our page and text for our Algolia search index.

The audio file also has more information available. We need the URL and the size. The URL will be important for display and the feeds, and the size is important for our RSS feed. We also want to order our episodes in descending order by publication date to allow for the proper flow of content:

```
query HygraphData {
  episodes(orderBy: publishDate_DESC) {
    audioFile {
      id
      url
      size
    }
    publishDate
    updatedAt
    slug
    title
    body {
      html
      text
    }}
  }
}
```

If you wish to explore further, you can use the playground explorer to see additional variations and data for each episode.

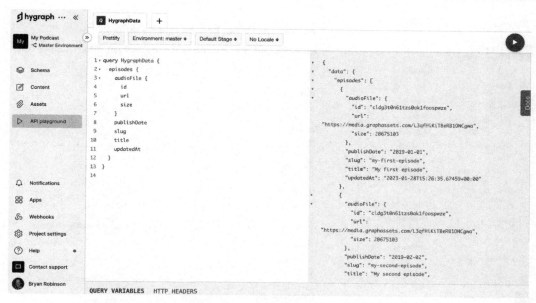

Figure 9.8 – The query and response inside Hygraph's API playground

We know how to query for the data we need, but now we need to open that data to use as an API.

Setting up Hygraph API access

To turn on API access, we need to head to the **Settings** area in the navigation pane. From there, we can navigate to the **API Access** page. This presents us with all the various endpoints. The main endpoint we'll need is **Content API**. We can go ahead and copy that URL and put it in our project's .env file alongside the Algolia environment variables. Setting this as an environment variable will make our code more portable later on. Give it the key HYGRAPH_ENDPOINT. When combined with the .env file of *Chapter 8*, your file should look like the following:

```
ALGOLIA_APP_ID="<app-id>"
ALGOLIA_API_KEY="<api-key>"
INDEX_NAME="episodes"
HYGRAPH_ENDPOINT="<endpoint url>"
```

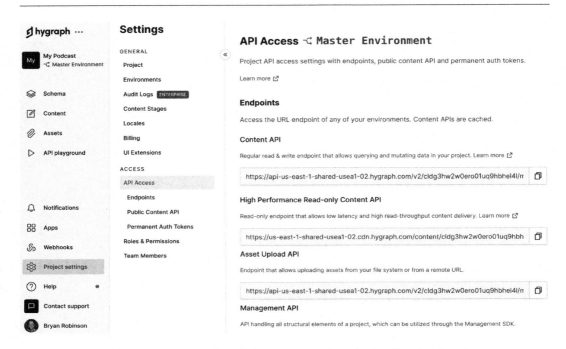

Figure 9.9: The API Access page has all the necessary API endpoints listed and ready to copy

This is the URL we need, but currently there are no permissions to query the API. Scroll further down the page to the **Public Content API** section. In this section, we can add permissions for the public API.

> **Public versus API tokens**
>
> If this were a sensitive API, we would want to set up specific API tokens to read this data, but as this is data we don't mind being public, setting it up as a Public API doesn't run too many risks and makes the process a bit easier.

To set the public API permissions, we can either set them granularly with the **Add permission** button or allow Hygraph to set defaults. The defaults will give read permissions to all models when the content has been published. This is what we want, so go with the defaults. If your needs change, you can always update this area with new permissions.

Public Content API

Configure public Content API access permissions for unauthenticated requests.

Default stage for public content delivery

If no stage parameter is set on the GraphQL query or additional HTTP header, then content from the selected default stage will be served. Learn more ☐

Published   Change default stage

⇅ Sort by: **Model: A to Z** ▾   + Filter permissions   + Add permission

Content Permissions   ⌄

ⓘ There are no public content API permissions set up.

Would you like us to initialize some defaults?

The defaults would allow unauthenticated users to:

Read   all models on stage   Published   for all locales

No, I'll configure custom permissions   Yes, initialize defaults

Figure 9.10: The Public Content API section with no permissions set

Once added, you'll be presented with the new permissions for the public content API.

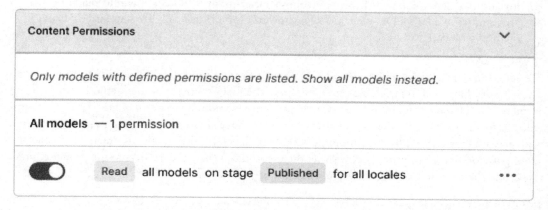

Content Permissions   ⌄

Only models with defined permissions are listed. Show all models instead.

All models — 1 permission

🔘   Read   all models on stage   Published   for all locales   •••

Figure 9.11: The Public Content API section after defaults have been added

With the permissions set and the API endpoint stored in our .env file, we're ready to query for the data in 11ty.

Querying and formatting the data for 11ty

If you remember all the way back to *Chapter 2*, you'll recall that we can add data to 11ty's Data Cascade in many different ways. The two ways that work best for the application of a headless CMS are a global JavaScript data file and configuration-generated global data. We've covered JavaScript data files a couple of times already in the book, so for this project, let's add this data via the configuration file.

Adding data via the `addGlobalData` method on the `eleventyConfig` option will add global data to our cascade that we can use with the added benefit of allowing this to be added to a plugin, as we'll discover in the next chapter.

The `addGlobalData` method accepts two arguments: a string to create the data key, and a function to return the data. In this case, we'll call our data `hygraph` and use an async function to fetch that data:

```
eleventyConfig.addGlobalData("hygraph", async function(){
 // Our function
}
```

The function needs to send the GraphQL query we wrote in the last section to Hygraph, decode the response to the JSON data, and then send that data to the Data Cascade.

Fetch request versus GraphQL NPM package

While there are many packages that allow you to send GraphQL queries to APIs, we can use a JavaScript `fetch` with the query as our body to accomplish this as well, without the need for another dependency. If I were putting together many API calls, I would reach for the ergonomics of a GraphQL query package; however for a single call, the standard `fetch()` method will work just fine.

To send the request, we'll create our query as a variable, and send that as the body to the Hygraph API. To do that, we'll use the `fetch()` method. The first argument of the method is the URL to send the HTTP request to. In this case, we can put our API endpoint as a string or add it to our `.env` file for greater portability. Since we're already set up to have environment variables from *Chapter 8*, let's go with that method for maximum portability of the code. The second argument is an object of configuration options. In this case, we'll set the method to `POST`, the headers to the proper content type, and the body to a stringified version of our query variable.

From there, we need to get the response as a JSON object, and then we can return the data object from that JSON. This will contain the `episodes` array but could also have other data if we sent additional queries in the `HygraphData` query:

```
eleventyConfig.addGlobalData("hygraph", async function(){
    const query = `query HygraphData {
        episodes(orderBy: publishDate_DESC) {
            audioFile {
```

```
              id
              url
              size
            }
            publishDate
            updatedAt
            slug
            title
            body {
              html
              text
            }
          }
        }
      }`
    const response = await fetch(process.
      env.HYGRAPH_ENDPOINT, {
        method: 'POST',
        headers: {
            'Content-Type': 'application/json',
        },
        body: JSON.stringify({query})

    })
    const json = await response.json()
    return json.data
  })
```

> **Warning: Node.js and fetch**
>
> The latest versions of Node.js have the `fetch` method built in. If you're following along in the technical requirements of the book from *Chapter 1*, you'll be using Node.js 18. If you are using previous versions, the `fetch` method won't be available. There are two methods to fix this in your project. First, you could upgrade to Node.js 18. If that's not possible for you, there's a package called `node-fetch` on NPM. It provides the exact syntax and functionality we need for our project. You'll need to run `npm install node-fetch` and create a variable in the `eleventy.config.js` file as `const fetch = require('node-fetch')`.

With that, all the episodes will be globally available with the `hygraph.episodes` key. We can now use this new data to replace our Markdown collection data with the new data being fetched from Hygraph. In the next section, we'll go through our project's pages and replace the references to the Markdown with references to this new data.

Converting existing pages to use CMS data

We have a series of pages that need to have their content updated with the new data source. Anywhere in the project that we loop through `collections.episodes`, we need to replace this with information from the `hygraph.episodes` array.

Both the `index.html` file and `episodes.html` have a simple loop that needs to be replaced. Aside from needing to change the source of the data, we also need to adjust the variables used. While collection item data is stored under a `data` key, this new data is directly in the `episode` object. We also need to format the slug to use the `/episodes/` prefix to link properly:

```
{% for episode in hygraph.episodes %}
    <h3><a href="/episodes/{{
    episode.slug }}">
        {{ episode.title }}
    </a></h3>
{% endfor %}
```

Next, we need to update the JSON file that we use to form our Algolia search index: `/src/algoliaIndex.njk`. This follows a similar pattern. Each variable will need to be replaced without the data key, and two additional changes need to happen:

- The episode URL needs to be updated to properly have the `/episodes/` URL.

- The content for Algolia needed filters to properly work with the content variable we used before. Now, we can use the `body.text` variable to get the plain text representation of our content. There is no more need for the filters we created in the previous chapter:

```
---
permalink: 'algoliaIndex.json'
---

[
{% for episode in hygraph.episodes %}
{%- set fullUrl = "/episodes/" + episode.slug %}
{%- set absolutePostUrl = fullUrl | absoluteUrl(site.url) %}


    {
        "objectID": "{{ episode.slug }}",
        "title": "{{ episode.title }}",
        "date": "{{ episode.publishDate }}",
        "url": "{{ absolutePostUrl }}",
        "content": "{{ episode.body.text }}"

    }{% if not loop.last %},{% endif %}
{% endfor %}
]
```

The final thing that needs to be updated is the RSS feed. This needs a little more work. Open the / src/feed.njk file to make these changes.

Two areas have information that we need from Hygraph: the latest episode's updated date (for the overall feed updated time), and the loop that creates each item for the feed. The latest episode no longer needs a filter. Our JSON data is now ordered by descending publish date, so we always know the latest episode. Instead of a filter, we can just get the first item of the episodes array and get the publish date.

This is the previous code:

```
<updated>{{ collections.episodes |
  getNewestCollectionItemDate | dateToRfc822 }}</updated>
```

This is the new code:

```
<updated>{{ hygraph.episodes[0].publishDate |
  dateToRfc822  }}</updated>
```

When you add that to your feed file, however, you'll get a new error. The publish date isn't coming through in a format that the RSS plugin understands as a date. To fix this, we can create a simple template filter to transform the date from Hygraph into a pure JavaScript date object.

> **Transforming the data**
>
> It's possible to also correct this when we're importing the data in our configuration file. That process works but adds a lot of data manipulation to how the data is fetched and stored. Manipulating it at the template level is safer and more in keeping with 11ty's overall philosophy.

In the eleventy.config.js configuration file, we can add a new filter that will take the date string from the Hygraph data and create a JavaScript date object and return that back. This format is what the RSS plugin expects, and we can then order our filters properly and get the correctly formatted date for our RSS feed. Note also that instead of having to use the Podcast Tools plugin to get the size of the audio file, we can now get that directly from the API. The power of a fully fledged API is great.

Add this filter to your eleventy.config.js file:

```
eleventyConfig.addFilter("jsDate", function(dateString) {
    return new Date(dateString);
});
```

Update the /src/feed.njk line we just updated with the filter we just added:

```
<updated>{{ hygraph.episodes[0].publishDate | jsDate |
dateToRfc822  }}</updated>
```

Then we can update the loop further along the feed template. This also will need the jsDate filter, as well as the new URL logic we created for the Algolia index:

```
{% for episode in hygraph.episodes %}
    {%- set fullUrl = "/episodes/" + episode.slug  %}
    {%- set absolutePostUrl = fullUrl | absoluteUrl
      (site.url) %}
    {%- set audioPath = episode.audioFile.url -%}
    <item>
<enclosure
    url="{{absolutePostUrl}}"
    length="{{ episode.audioFile.size }}"
    type="audio/mpeg"
/>
    <title>{{ episode.title }}</title>
    <link href="{{ absolutePostUrl }}" />
    <updated>{{ episode.updatedAt | jsDate | dateToRfc822
      }}</updated>
    <id>{{ absolutePostUrl }}</id>
    <content type="html">
      <![CDATA[
    {{ episode.body.html }}
    ]]>
    </content>
    </item>
  {% endfor %}
```

Now we have a functioning home page, episodes page, Algolia index, and RSS feed. We don't have individual pages generated from the Hygraph data. To fix this, we can use 11ty's Pagination API.

Creating a pagination template to create individual 11ty pages

While it may seem counterintuitive to use something named Pagination to create individual pieces of content, that's where the power of 11ty's Pagination API comes into play. We can use it in this way, as well as creating standard pagination. Instead of having a set number of items per page, we can specify one item at a time, thus creating individual pages for our data.

We begin as we did with pagination in *Chapter 4*, but instead of having 5 or 10 items per page, we set that to 1. Then we can also create specific URLs for the pages by using the permalink functionality set to the slug of each item. We also need a title for the templates we've already created as well as audioURL to function properly. Instead of rewriting our templates, we can set this information with the eleventyComputed object to create the variables using the data that we receive.

From there, we need to provide the proper page content. The two changes here will be the audio player and body content HTML that the Hygraph API provides us from the Rich Text field. We can add all of this into a new page template named hygraphEpisodes.html. In this case, the filename doesn't matter, as we'll generate the URL from the permalink data:

```
---
pagination:
  data: hygraph.episodes
  size: 1
  alias: episode
permalink: "/episodes/{{ episode.slug }}/"
layout: "layouts/base.html"
eleventyComputed:
  title: "{{ episode.title }}"
  audioUrl: "{{ episode.audioFile.url }}"
---

{% include 'includes/player.html' %}

{{ episode.body.html }}
```

After this template is created, we can safely delete the episodes directory, as we no longer need the Markdown in that directory or the data in its JSON data file.

There's one last problem to fix. Now that the data for our episodes is no longer stored in GitHub, there's no longer a way to republish the site when a new episode is added.

To fix that, we can use webhooks functionality provided by both Hygraph and our hosting provider – in this case, Netlify.

Setting up a publication flow with webhooks

To start, we need a URL to send a webhook to when content is published in Hygraph. A webhook is a mechanism where a service sends a request when something happens within that service. The request can run and trigger other services to do various actions. In this example, Hygraph will send out a request when content is published. The request will go to Netlify and trigger a build so that our site has fresh content.

To do that, we can go to our host and use a build hook. This functionality may be named differently in each host, but this is what Netlify calls the functionality. This is a URL that a request can be sent to and have Netlify rebuild the site.

To set this up, we need to add some additional information in Netlify and Hygraph:

1. Navigate to your project's Netlify **Site Settings** and go to the **Build and Deploy** settings. This page has a section titled **Build hooks**:

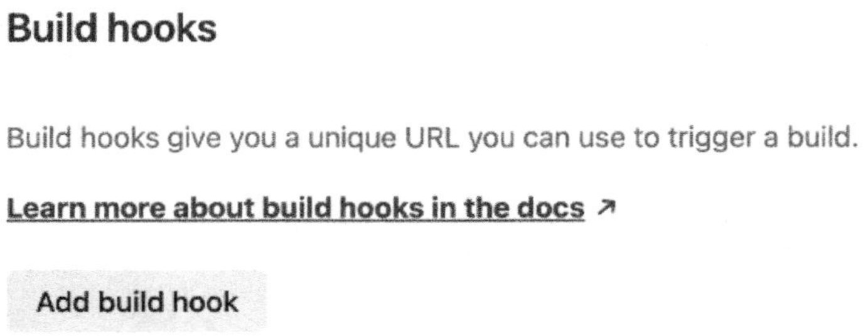

    ## Build hooks

    Build hooks give you a unique URL you can use to trigger a build.

    Learn more about build hooks in the docs ↗

    Add build hook

    Figure 9.12 – The Build hooks interface in Netlify's project settings

2. Add a build hook named `Hygraph Content`. This will let us know what triggered a build when it happened.

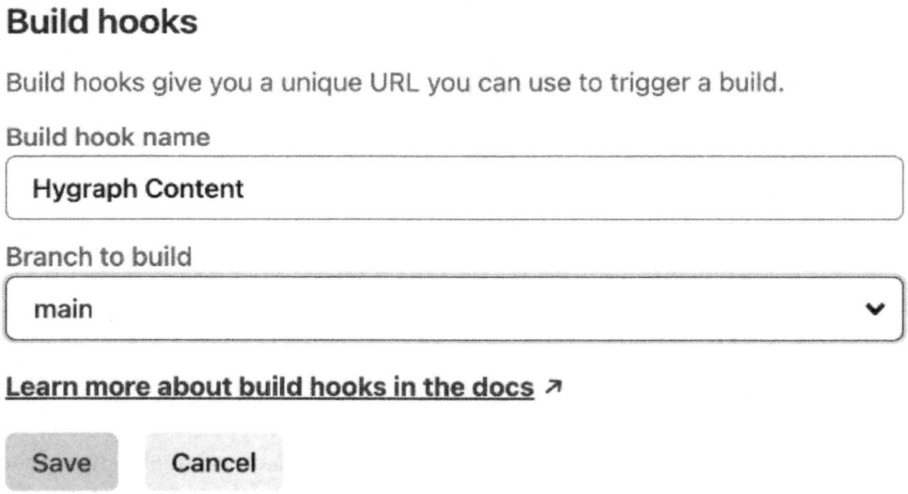

    ## Build hooks

    Build hooks give you a unique URL you can use to trigger a build.

    Build hook name

    > Hygraph Content

    Branch to build

    > main   ⌄

    Learn more about build hooks in the docs ↗

    Save   Cancel

    Figure 9.13 – The build hook settings

3. Save that hook, and it will give us a URL named **Hygraph Content**:

Build hooks

Build hooks give you a unique URL you can use to trigger a build.

Hygraph Content: https://api.netlify.com/build_hooks/63d6d60f82137510ec234c4a

Learn more about build hooks in the docs ↗

Add build hook

Figure 9.14 – The completed build hook with a URL

4. We can take this URL to Hygraph and set up a webhook for when content is updated or created. In the main navigation of our project, there's a **Webhooks** page. Click **Add webhook** to create a new webhook for use.

Webhooks

Webhooks are a fundamental method for observing changes that happen to content within your project.

Learn more ↗

Figure 9.15 – The Webhooks interface in Hygraph

5. Give it a name and the URL provided by Netlify. In this case, we don't need a payload, since we're just telling Netlify to rebuild the site. We then need to adjust the triggers. We want to trigger the deployment when an asset (image or audio) or episode is saved into the **Published** stage or **Unpublished** stage.

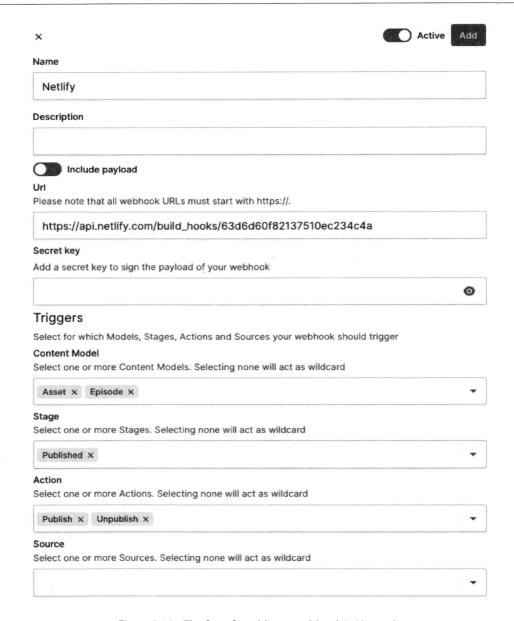

Figure 9.16 – The form for adding a webhook in Hygraph

With this, any time content is published or unpublished in our Hygraph project, the site will rebuild. When the site is rebuilding, it will query Hygraph and get all the up-to-date information to build the site.

Now we have a fully functional, headless-CMS-driven 11ty website.

Summary

In this chapter, we went through what it takes to hook your 11ty website up to a headless CMS. This gives us the ability to have a solid editing experience without sacrificing our developer experience. In fact, with some of the extra features that come with a CMS, we were able to remove the need for some instances of 11ty plugins.

To move to the CMS, we created our content model inside Hygraph. The content model lined up with the data we needed for our 11ty site. We created content inside of Hygraph and we created a query to get the content data via GraphQL inside Hygraph's API playground. From there, we used 11ty's configuration data API to fetch the data and changed our templates to use that data instead of the collection data. From there, the site was using the headless CMS, but we still wanted a seamless deployment, so we used webhooks in Hygraph and build hooks in Netlify to create a flow for when content is added or updated in Hygraph to build the site again in our host Netlify.

In the next chapter, we'll wrap up much of what we've worked on in this book by exploring plugin creation and making a plugin that contains many of the helper functions we've used in these projects for use in new projects going forward.

Creating Custom 11ty Plugins

In this book, we've created four separate projects that have put 11ty through its paces. While most of it has been a fun exercise in coding, doing the same tasks over and over again in your regular work is less efficient than is optimal. In this chapter, we'll take much of the knowledge earned in the course of this book and put it all together into a series of 11ty plugins that you can use in any of your projects and publish for others to use, as well.

We've used plugins multiple times throughout the book but haven't dived into what it takes to make one. The process is not too different from the work we've done in creating sites with 11ty. In this chapter, we'll discuss what a plugin is, and convert reusable features from our various projects into individual plugins. To do that, we'll cover plugin basic setup, plugin testing, and creating plugin configuration options in the following sections:

- What can an 11ty plugin do?

- Creating a basic plugin

- Creating a configurable data source plugin

- Creating an Algolia helper plugin that can read from a project's files

- Publishing your plugin

Technical requirements

This project has a little less setup than the full website projects we've built in this book. We want to keep the plugin directories as clean as possible. As usual, there's a project folder in the book's GitHub repository at `https://github.com/PacktPublishing/Eleventy-by-Example` that has a solid starting point for each plugin. You'll also want access to the previous projects' code, as we'll be using code we've already written to create these plugins.

Each plugin we create in this chapter starts from a basic file structure. While we covered best practice project structure in *Chapter 1*, those best practices were for websites. We want each of these plugins to have as little configuration as possible, so we use the default 11ty structure. Because of this, we don't have an `src` directory and don't rearrange the layouts and includes separately. The basic project structure for each is a `package.json` file starting with just 11ty, a simple `index.md` file, and an `_includes` directory that contains the base template for the home page. This requires no configuration to accomplish.

What can an 11ty plugin do?

An 11ty plugin is, at its core, a portable configuration file that can be installed via npm into new projects. Each plugin defines a set of functionality in the `eleventy.config.js` file.

Anything possible in a regular 11ty project is possible in an 11ty plugin, such as the following:

- Custom filters
- Custom shortcodes
- Global data creation
- 11ty events
- Custom template language support (e.g., adding Sass support or JavaScript compiling support)
- 11ty output transformations (e.g., minifying HTML)
- Conditionally adding or removing files

Anything you can do from within the `eleventy.config.js` file is possible. While the preceding list has many common use cases, there are plenty more. After going through the examples in this chapter, set your sights on other common use cases that you'd like to streamline for yourself.

Let's start by creating a basic plugin to allow a project to have access to three shortcodes.

Creating a basic plugin

For our first example plugin, let's take the multimedia shortcodes we created in *Chapter 5* and convert them into a plugin.

Basic setup

To start, we need to configure our `package.json` file to be ready for inclusion in external projects. Give your plugin a name and description that will help users find it, and give it a proper version number. In this case, our media shortcode will start at a very low version number. When initializing an npm package, by default, the `main` variable will be `index.js`. This is the main file the package expects to run. Our main file isn't `index.js` but instead `eleventy.config.js`. This is so we can run 11ty inside this plugin for testing purposes and external projects can ingest the code properly, as well.

For all the plugins in this chapter, the `package.json` file should be very similar with the only differences being additional npm packages that need to be installed:

```json
{
  "name": "eleventy-plugin-media-helpers",
  "version": "0.0.1",
  "description": "",
  "main": "eleventy.config.js",
  "scripts": {
    "dev": "eleventy --serve",
    "build": "eleventy"
  },
  "keywords": [],
  "author": "",
  "license": "ISC",
  "dependencies": {
    "@11ty/eleventy": "^2.0.0"
  }
}
```

All the functionality of our plugin will now need to live in `eleventy.config.js`. This file should be set up exactly the same as if we were configuring a new 11ty site. We export a function from this module file and pass it in the `eleventyConfig` object. This will give us all the functionality we'd normally have on our sites.

We can start testing our plugin project by running the following command in the project directory in your terminal:

```
npm run dev
```

This should be very familiar to how we ran all our projects thus far. In this case, the home page will have a simple `h1` element. This is stored in the `index.html` file. This file is where we'll test all of our functionality.

Currently, we don't have any functionality except the basic 11ty functionality. Let's add some!

Creating shortcodes and testing

The functionality of our plugin will reside within the `eleventy.config.js` configuration file. For this plugin, we want to copy the following functionality from *Chapter 5*'s code:

- YouTube shortcode
- CodePen shortcode
- Blockquote shortcode

These three basic shortcodes and their dependencies are all we need to get from the configuration file of *Chapter 5*.

The final configuration file should look like the following (for a detailed breakdown of how these shortcodes function, read *Chapter 5*):

```
module.exports = function(eleventyConfig) {
    eleventyConfig.addShortcode("youtube", (id, title=
"A YouTube Video") => {
        return `<iframe
            style="aspect-ratio: 16 / 9; width: 100%"
            src="https://www.youtube.com/embed/${id}"
            title="${title}"
            frameborder="0"
            allow="accelerometer; autoplay;
                clipboard-write; encrypted-media;
                    gyroscope; picture-in-picture"
            allowfullscreen></iframe>`
    })

    eleventyConfig.addPairedShortcode("codepen",
        ( content, url, tabs="html,result",
            theme="default", height="300"  ) => {
        // split and name all the parts of the url from
            codepen
        const [ protocol, , domain, user, pen, hash ] =
            url.split("/");

        const markup = `<div class="codepen"
        data-height="${height}"
        data-theme-id="${theme}"
        data-default-tab="${tabs}"
        data-slug-hash="${hash}"
        data-user="${user}"
        style="box-sizing: border-box; display: flex;
            flex-direction: column; align-items: center;
                justify-content: center; border: 2px solid;
                    margin: 1em 0; padding: 1em;">
                <h3>Your JS is turned off. Please turn it on to
                    see the codepen. Here's a screenshot from
                        <a href="${url}">the Pen</a></h3>
                <a href="${url}"><img style="max-width:
                    100%;box-shadow: 1px 1px 5px #999;"
                        src="${url}/image/large.png" /></a>
                ${content}
```

```
      </div>
      <script async src="https://cpwebassets.codepen.io
        /assets/embed/ei.js"></script>
      `;
      return markup
   })

   eleventyConfig.addPairedShortcode("blockquote",
     (content, author, cite, float=false) => {
       const markup = `
       <figure class="blockquote ${float ?
         `float-${float}` : ""}">
           <blockquote>
               ${content}
           </blockquote>
           <figcaption class="blockquote cite">
               By ${author} in <cite>${cite}</cite>
           </figcaption>
       </figure>`
       return markup
   })
}
```

Once this is updated, all three shortcodes are available for use on the plugin's site. Let's do the minimum test case. Update the index.html file to use each shortcode:

```
---
layout: "base.html"
---

# Eleventy Plugin Media Helpers Test

## YouTube Test

{% youtube "x8jcqvsC4cY" %}

## Codepen test

{% codepen "https://codepen.io/brob/pen/bMqBgb" %}
This is a test of the codepen shortcode
{% endcodepen %}

## Blockquote test
```

```
{% blockquote "Bryan Robinson" "Blog Thing" %}
This is a blockquote
{% endblockquote %}
```

Now we have an embedded YouTube video, CodePen demo, and blockquote all on the home page.

Eleventy Plugin Media Helpers Test

YouTube Test

Codepen test

Blockquote test

> This is a blockquote

By Bryan Robinson in *Blog Thing*

Figure 10.1 – The plugin displaying a YouTube video, a CodePen embed, and a blockquote

These work in this test project, but how can we test this without publishing it to npm first? Let's test this plugin with *Chapter 5*'s end site.

Testing the plugin in a real project

While bundling this into an npm package may feel like the next step, we need to make sure this plugin will work in a real project first. Let's test this against the end code of *Project 2*.

Navigate in the book's GitHub repository to `project-2/chapter-5/end`. Start this project with `npm run dev` and then let's work on updating the project to use the new local version of the plugin.

In the future, we would install the plugin by installing the npm package and then requiring that package in the configuration file.

Instead, we can require the directory from our local computer. To start, remove the three shortcodes and their dependencies from the site's `eleventy.config.js` file. This should break the running site, as 11ty can no longer find the custom shortcodes:

```js
const dynamicCategories = require('eleventy-plugin-dynamic-
categories');

module.exports = function(eleventyConfig) {
    // Set the collection to reverse chronological order
    eleventyConfig.addCollection("post", (collection) => {
        return collection.getFilteredByTag
            ("post").reverse();
    });
    eleventyConfig.addPlugin(dynamicCategories, {
        categoryVar: "categories", // Name of your category
        variable from your frontmatter (default: categories)
        itemsCollection: "post", // Name of your collection
            to use for the items (default: posts)
        perPageCount: 10 // Items per page of your
            paginated category (default: 5)
    })

    // Copy `assets/` to `_site/assets/`
    eleventyConfig.addPassthroughCopy("assets");

    // Set the source for 11ty to the /src directory
    // Otherwise, this defaults to the project root
    // This provides a cleaner project structure
    return {
        dir: {
            input: "src",
            output: "_site", // This is the default,
```

```
                but it's included here for clarity.
            includes: "_templates"
        }
    }
}
```

Next, we need to add the plugin. At the top of the file, start by requiring the package with a relative path to where the plugin lives on your computer in relation to the site's directory. If you're in the full GitHub repository, the following code should work by navigating back up the file tree to where the new plugin lives in `project-5`:

```
const mediaPlugin = require
    ('../../../project-5/end/eleventy-plugin-media-helpers')
```

From here, we can initialize the plugin like the ones we've done in previous chapters:

```
eleventyConfig.addPlugin(mediaPlugin)
```

Once this is in the exported function, we can restart the 11ty server and all the media we have in our blog posts in the project should work just like they did when reading the information from the site's configuration, except now it's reading it from our plugin.

This works for all the basic functionality of 11ty, but what if we need to have different information for each project? That's where creating a set of configurable options comes in. Let's set up a new plugin to create the Hygraph data from *Chapter 9* for new projects.

Creating a configurable data source plugin for Hygraph data

We set up our Hygraph data in *Chapter 9* to read from a specific Hygraph project with a specific GraphQL query. Not every project will need to use that same project and that same query. How can we configure a plugin to dynamically change the Hygraph endpoint, query, and data key for each new project?

We can set this up with configuration options.

Setting up the plugin to accept options

To start, let's move to the `eleventy-plugin-hygraph-data` directory and run 11ty from within that project. This has the same initial setup as our last plugin: index file, simple included template, and blank configuration. Let's start by setting up the options in our configuration file.

When being used as a plugin, the exported function of the `eleventy.config.js` file will be an optional `options` object that a user can pass in when using the `addPlugin` method in their configuration. To begin, add that argument and then we'll create a set of defaults that we can use in the test code, as well as make sure any required data is set.

For the Hygraph plugin, we'll want to make the data key, endpoint, and query all configurable, since projects will have different needs for these. Then, we need to merge this object with the `options` object to ensure the right data gets used:

```
module.exports = function(eleventyConfig, options) {
    const defaults = {
        dataKey: "hygraph",
        endpoint: process.env.HYGRAPH_ENDPOINT,
        query: `query HygraphData {
            episodes(orderBy: publishDate_DESC) {
                title
            }
        }`
    }
    const combinedOptions = {
        ...defaults,
        ...options
    }
    // ... The rest of the configuration
}
```

Once the defaults and options are in place, we can use the `addGlobalData` function that we used in *Chapter 9* to pull in Hygraph data. Instead of using the environment variables and hardcoded strings, we need to convert each to the new `combinedOptions` variables:

```
require('dotenv').config();

module.exports = function(eleventyConfig, options) {
    const defaults = {
        dataKey: "hygraph",
        endpoint: your-hygraph-endpoint,
        query: `query HygraphData {
            episodes(orderBy: publishDate_DESC) {
                title
            }
        }`
    }

    const combinedOptions = {
        ...defaults,
        ...options
    }
    eleventyConfig.addGlobalData(combinedOptions.dataKey,
        async function(){
        const response = await fetch(combinedOptions.
            endpoint, {
```

```
        method: 'POST',
        headers: {
            'Content-Type': 'application/json',
        },
        body: JSON.stringify({query: combinedOptions.
            query})
    })
    const json = await response.json()
    return json.data
    })
}
```

Save this, and we should now have a new object in our global data with a key of `hygraph`. Let's test this in our index file, by looping through the episodes that should exist:

```
---
layout: "base.html"
---


# Eleventy Plugin Hygraph Data Test

{% for episode in hygraph.episodes %}
    {{ episode.title }}
{% endfor %}
```

To test in a real project, let's follow the same path as before and test against `project-4/chapter-9`'s end directory.

Eleventy Plugin Hygraph Data Test

My second episode

My first episode

Figure 10.2 – Very simple output from the Hygraph plugin showing
the two episodes we created in Chapter 9

Testing the configuration

Navigate in the repository to `/project-4/chapter-9/end`. Run `npm run dev` in this directory and open up the `eleventy.config.js` file. In this file, remove the `addGlobalData` method, which is currently how the project populates episodes from Hygraph. Just like in the last example, this will break 11ty.

Require the new plugin at the top as we did before, and then add it with the new `options` object being passed as the second argument. This object should have keys corresponding to the defaults we set in the plugin. Once this is saved, the site should build again, as we're now pulling in all the Hygraph data we need:

```
// ... Additional require statements removed for brevity
const hygraphDataPlugin = require
    ('../../../project-5/end/eleventy-plugin-hygraph-data')
module.exports = function(eleventyConfig) {
    eleventyConfig.addPlugin(hygraphDataPlugin, {
        dataKey: "hygraph",
        endpoint: process.env.HYGRAPH_ENDPOINT,
        query: `query HygraphData {
            episodes(orderBy: publishDate_DESC) {
                audioFile {
                    id
                    url
                    size
                }
                publishDate
                updatedAt
                slug
                title
                body {
                    html
                    text
                }
            }
        }`
    })
```

Now, we have a fully functioning data plugin that allows any project to query any Hygraph project with a configurable query to add the needed data!

Finally, let's consolidate a little more from *Project 4* and create a plugin to handle our Algolia search needs, as well.

Creating an Algolia helper plugin that can read from a project's files

This plugin has a lot of work to do. We have three simple filters to add, a complex filter, and an event that we can use to send the JSON data from a project to Algolia.

Let's get things set up as before. Navigate to the final plugin directory of this project, `/project-5/ start/eleventy-plugin-algolia-helper`, and run the project. Then, let's add our simple filters from *Chapter 8* – `jsDate`, `jsonify`, and `htmlStrip`:

```
module.exports = function(eleventyConfig, options) {
    eleventyConfig.addFilter
        ("jsDate", function(dateString) {
        return new Date(dateString);
    });

    eleventyConfig.addFilter("jsonify", function(content) {
        return JSON.stringify(content);
    })

    eleventyConfig.addFilter("htmlStrip", (content) => {
        return content.replace(/(<([^>]+)>)/gi, "");
    })
}
```

We can test these just like before with the `index.md` file in the plugin directory. Since these are doing data manipulation, we'll create some data in the frontmatter and show the raw data and the output data:

```
---
layout: "base.html"
data:
  html: <h1 class="myClass">Test</h1><p>Test</p>
  date: "2020-01-01"
---


# Eleventy Plugin Algolia Helper Test

## Remove HTML
### Raw data
```
  {{ data.html }}
```


### Using | htmlStrip

```
  {{ data.html | htmlStrip }}
```
```

```
## jsDate
### Raw data
```

  {{ data.date }}
```

### Using | jsDate

```

  {{ data.date | jsDate }}
```


## jsonify

### Raw data

```

  {{ data }}
```


### Using | jsonify

```

  {{ data | jsonify }}
```


## search

```

  {{ "test" | search | jsonify }}
```
```

Each of the filters should output the appropriate data.

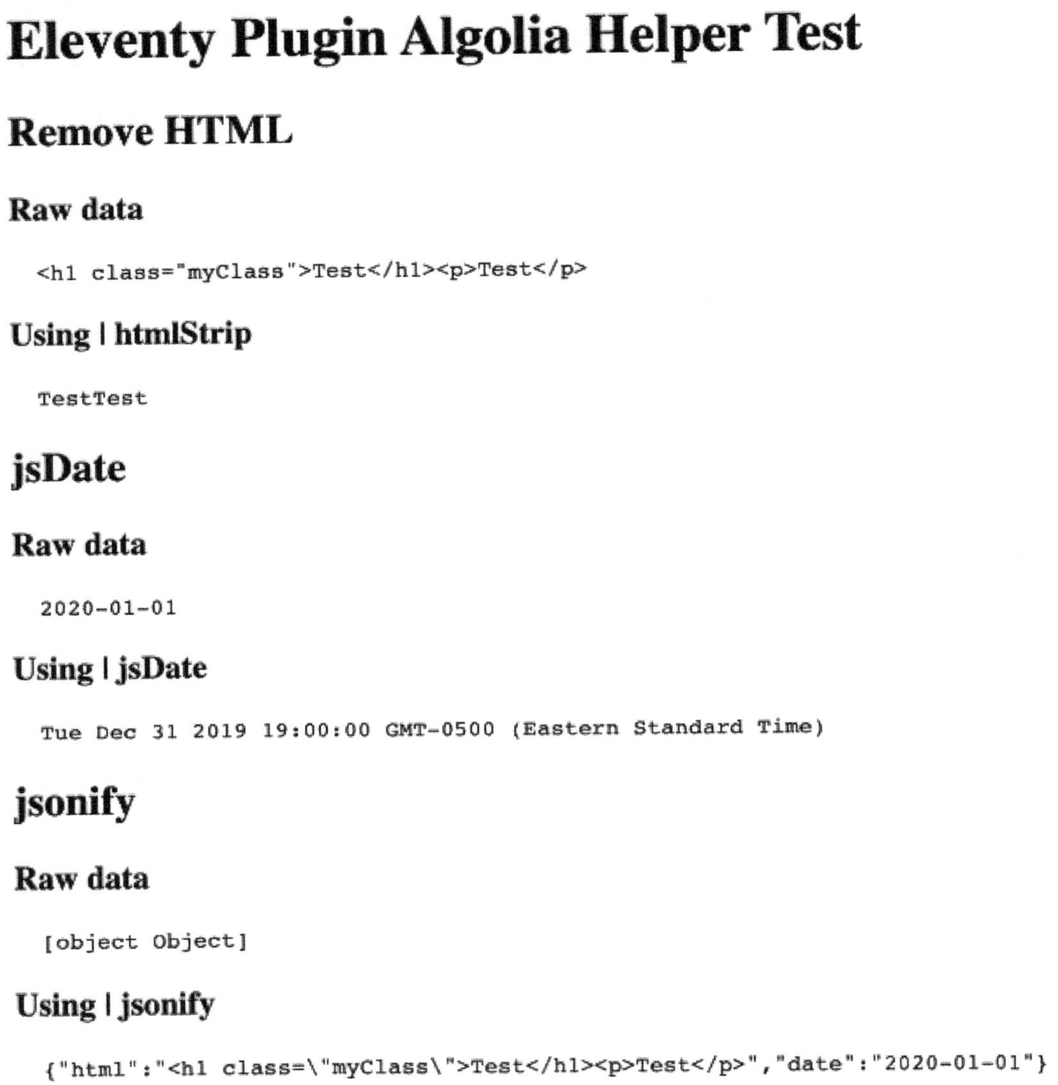

Eleventy Plugin Algolia Helper Test

Remove HTML

Raw data

```
<h1 class="myClass">Test</h1><p>Test</p>
```

Using | htmlStrip

```
TestTest
```

jsDate

Raw data

```
2020-01-01
```

Using | jsDate

```
Tue Dec 31 2019 19:00:00 GMT-0500 (Eastern Standard Time)
```

jsonify

Raw data

```
[object Object]
```

Using | jsonify

```
{"html":"<h1 class=\"myClass\">Test</h1><p>Test</p>","date":"2020-01-01"}
```

Figure 10.3 – The output of the Algolia test page with data displaying and being transformed by the filters

This all looks good.

Next, we want to have the search filter for running our Algolia searches. To start, we need to install the `algoliasearch` npm package for use in the plugin:

```
npm install algoliasearch
```

Then, we'll create `options` and `defaults` objects, like in the Hygraph plugin. In this case, we need the Algolia App ID, API key, index name, and the attributes we want to return for the search. All of these should be configurable per project:

```
module.exports = function(eleventyConfig, options) {
    const defaults = {
        appId: <your-app-id>,
        apiKey: <your-api-key>,
        indexName: <your-index-name>,
        attributesToRetrieve: ["title", "url"],
    }

    const combinedOptions = {
        ...defaults,
        ...options
    }
    // ... The rest of the file
}
```

We can then use these in the filter instead of hardcoded values or environment variables:

```
    eleventyConfig.addFilter("search", (query) => {
        const algoliasearchlite = require
            ('algoliasearch/lite')
        const client = algoliasearchlite
            (combinedOptions.appId, combinedOptions.apiKey);
        const index = client.initIndex
            (combinedOptions.indexName);
        return index.search(query, {
            attributesToRetrieve: combinedOptions
                .attributesToRetrieve,

        }).then(res => {
            return res.hits;
        })
    })
```

Once that's in place, we can test locally. While we used this in an 11ty serverless template in *Chapter 8*, we can test the plugin with a simple string:

```
## search

```
    {{ "test" | search | jsonify }}
```
```

Once saved, the search results should come back with any hits from the string `test`.

search

```
[{"title":"My second episode","url":"https://mypodcast.com/episodes/my-second-episode/","objectID":"my-second-episode",
```

Figure 10.4 – The search filter displaying the search object from Algolia

So, we have our three helper filters, and a filter to do the query. What about the functionality to ingest a JSON file into Algolia?

We can do that with the plugin as well.

We need two new options for this: a Boolean to check whether we should run indexing, and where the index file lives in the project. For our defaults, we can use `true` and `false`, but for the real plugin use, we'll use a conditional to return the proper Boolean for whatever use case we have:

```
const defaults = {
    appId: process.env.ALGOLIA_APP_ID,
    apiKey: process.env.ALGOLIA_API_KEY,
    indexName: process.env.INDEX_NAME,
    attributesToRetrieve: ["title", "url"],
    shouldRunIndexing: false,
    indexFile: "_site/index.json",
}
```

We'll start the event, much like we did in *Chapter 8*, but we'll add a few console logs to give some assurance on when the indexing is running or not running. The rest of the code will go forward much like *Chapter 8*, but with the new `option` variables instead of hardcoded values:

```
eleventyConfig.on('eleventy.after', async () => {
    const algoliasearch = require('algoliasearch')

    console.log("Checking to see if we should run
        indexing")
    if (!combinedOptions.shouldRunIndexing) {
        console.log("Option shouldRunIndexing is false,
            so not running indexing")
        return
    }
    console.log("Running indexing")

    // Need to know where the index file is
    // The context of the plugin is the plugin
        directory, so this won't work
    const jsonContent = await require
        (combinedOptions.indexFile)
```

```
        const client = algoliasearch(combinedOptions.appId,
            combinedOptions.apiKey);
        const index = client.initIndex
            (combinedOptions.indexName);

        index.saveObjects(jsonContent)
        console.log("Indexing complete")
    });
```

This code doesn't quite work yet, however. The working directory for the plugin is not the working path for our project. The `combinedOptions.indexFile` variable is not right. We could make the project developer provide a full path here, but that would be more overhead than what a plugin should require. Instead, we can use a function from within 11ty's utilities to find the current project's working directory. The `TemplatePath` object in `eleventy-utils` has a method called `getWorkingDir()`, which will return the absolute path to the current project. Combine that with the option of the file path to the index file, and we now have a working indexing event:

```
eleventyConfig.on('eleventy.after', async () => {
    const algoliasearch = require('algoliasearch')
    const { TemplatePath } = require
        ("@11ty/eleventy-utils");


    console.log("Checking to see if we should
        run indexing")
    if (!combinedOptions.shouldRunIndexing) {
        console.log("Option shouldRunIndexing is false,
            so not running indexing")
        return
    }
    console.log("Running indexing")

    const jsonContent = await require
        (TemplatePath.getWorkingDir() +
            combinedOptions.indexFile)

    const client = algoliasearch(combinedOptions.appId,
        combinedOptions.apiKey);
    const index = client.initIndex
        (combinedOptions.indexName);

    index.saveObjects(jsonContent)
    console.log("Indexing complete")
});
```

From here, test this as we have in the previous examples by removing all the functionality from *Chapter 8*'s end configuration and inserting this as a plugin.

These plugins are great, but they're only on our computers. This means we can't use them in our build process, and making them usable for our other projects is a chore. Let's get them ready for use as npm packages.

Publishing your plugin

Each plugin in the 11ty ecosystem is an npm package. That means we need to publish our plugin to npm. To publish a package on the npm registry, you'll need an account.

You can sign up for a free account at `npmjs.org`.

Once you have an account, you'll need to add the account to your local npm command line:

```
npm addUser
```

The `addUser` command will require a username and password and may also require two-factor authentication if that's set up on your npm account.

Once you have a user, you can publish your plugin, but the plugin will publish more than we want. We currently have all our test content. While, in this case, that's not a lot of files, our end users and projects don't need to download those files when they just want a functioning plugin.

To remove the files, we can add a `.npmignore` file to our directory. Those files can remain in GitHub if we use version control but won't be in the npm repository:

```
_site
.env
index.md
_includes
```

There's also no information on how to use the plugin. Creating a `ReadMe` file will go a long way toward easing a developer's path to using your plugin (even if that developer is just you in the future!).

The following structure is a great start toward creating your documentation. This comes from Stephanie Eckles' amazing 11ty plugin starter template (`https://github.com/5t3ph/eleventy-pl-ugin-template/blob/main/README.md#usage`):

```
## Usage

Describe how to install your plugin, such as:

```bash
npm install @scope/plugin-name
```
```

```
Then, include it in your `eleventy.config.js` config file:

```js
const pluginName = require("@scope/plugin-name");

module.exports = (eleventyConfig) => {
  eleventyConfig.addPlugin(pluginName);
};
```

Config Options

Option	Type	Default
option name	type	default value

Config Examples

Show examples of likely configurations.

Credits

Add credits if needed.
```

Once you have the documentation in place, make sure you fill out any information in your package.json file to give additional details and findability. Things like keywords and author information can help people discover the plugin. Including a license is also recommended so people know what to expect on using the plugin.

You'll note the verbose name of the package, as well. By convention, all 11ty plugins are prefixed with eleventy-plugin- to allow for additional findability in the npm registry. The name should also be unique, so if you're publishing one of these plugins, be sure to think through the name and create something different from the examples.

With all that done, run npm publish. Now, npm will ask you to log in and then it will publish your package.

The plugin is ready to be used by any 11ty developer.

Summary

In this chapter, we took all that we've learned through the book and created some reusable code in the form of 11ty plugins. We created a basic plugin that added the shortcodes we created in *Chapter 4*. We made configurable plugins to add Hygraph data for future projects, and we made an Algolia helper plugin that combined basic functionality, configurability, and the ability to find and manipulate files per project.

When creating functionality that you use over and over again, creating a plugin can be a great solution to reduce the amount of copying and pasting you have to do. It also helps grow the 11ty ecosystem. If you're looking for functionality, you can be sure someone else is as well. Publish your plugin to help them out!

More on plugins

Want to learn more about 11ty plugins? Watch this video from the *Learn with Jason* show to get more inspiration about what you can do with plugins: `https://www.learnwithjason.dev/create-a-plugin-for-11ty`

With that, we've been through the main functionality of creating websites with 11ty. From these five projects, you can extend the functionality to create many different types of sites with a focus on static-first performance.

In the fast-paced world of frontend development, 11ty may never be the most popular framework, but its flexibility is hard to beat, and the ability to only use features you need for a given project means you're never bloating your code or your users' browsers with additional features that aren't being used. It's a solid workhorse in your development arsenal.

I encourage you to work 11ty into your regular development tools and think static-first whenever possible.

Index

Packtpub.com

Subscribe to our online digital library for full access to over 7,000 books and videos, as well as industry leading tools to help you plan your personal development and advance your career. For more information, please visit our website.

Why subscribe?

- Spend less time learning and more time coding with practical eBooks and Videos from over 4,000 industry professionals

- Improve your learning with Skill Plans built especially for you

- Get a free eBook or video every month

- Fully searchable for easy access to vital information

- Copy and paste, print, and bookmark content

Did you know that Packt offers eBook versions of every book published, with PDF and ePub files available? You can upgrade to the eBook version at packtpub.com and as a print book customer, you are entitled to a discount on the eBook copy. Get in touch with us at customercare@packtpub.com for more details.

At www.packtpub.com, you can also read a collection of free technical articles, sign up for a range of free newsletters, and receive exclusive discounts and offers on Packt books and eBooks.

Other Books You May Enjoy

If you enjoyed this book, you may be interested in these other books by Packt:

Real-World Next.js

Michele Riva

ISBN: 978-1-80107-349-3

- Get up to speed with Next.js essentials and learn how to build apps quickly.
- Understand how to create scalable Next.js architectures.
- Write unit tests and integration tests in your Next.js application.
- Discover the powerful routing system and Next.js' built-in components.
- Design and build modern architectures with Next.js using GraphCMS or any headless CMS.

Elevating React Web Development with Gatsby

Samuel Larsen-Disney

ISBN: 978-1-80020-909-1

- Understand what GatsbyJS is, where it excels, and how to use it.
- Structure and build a GatsbyJS site with confidence.
- Elevate your site with an industry-standard approach to styling.
- Configure your GatsbyJS projects with search engine optimization to improve their ranking.
- Get to grips with advanced GatsbyJS concepts to create powerful and dynamic sites.

Packt is searching for authors like you

If you're interested in becoming an author for Packt, please visit `authors.packtpub.com` and apply today. We have worked with thousands of developers and tech professionals, just like you, to help them share their insight with the global tech community. You can make a general application, apply for a specific hot topic that we are recruiting an author for, or submit your own idea.

Hi!

I'm Bryan Robinson, author of *Eleventy by Example*. I really hope you enjoyed reading this book and found it useful for increasing your knowledge and understanding of static-first website building with 11ty.

If you learned something from the book, I would appreciate it if you could leave a review on Amazon sharing your thoughts. It helps others find the book and start their static-first journey.

Go to the link below or scan the QR code to leave your review: `https://packt.link/r/1804610496`

Your review will help us to understand what's worked well in this book, and what could be improved upon for future editions, so it really is appreciated.

Best wishes,

Download a free PDF copy of this book

Thanks for purchasing this book!

Do you like to read on the go but are unable to carry your print books everywhere?

Is your eBook purchase not compatible with the device of your choice?

Don't worry, now with every Packt book you get a DRM-free PDF version of that book at no cost.

Read anywhere, any place, on any device. Search, copy, and paste code from your favorite technical books directly into your application.

The perks don't stop there, you can get exclusive access to discounts, newsletters, and great free content in your inbox daily

Follow these simple steps to get the benefits:

1. Scan the QR code or visit the link below

https://packt.link/free-ebook/9781804610497

2. Submit your proof of purchase
3. That's it! We'll send your free PDF and other benefits to your email directly

collections - combine data from multiple sources into
a single entity.
e.g. "tags"
Uses the _collections dir and .js files
to define.

{ 1. _data (.json): readonly Set
{ 2. _pages (.md) → [{ head, content}]: readonly Set
              path
              matter
▸ 3. _collections (.js) { collection: data}

_series

Printed in Great Britain
by Amazon

22631308R00110